Secret Men's Bu.

What defines a middle-aged man?
Is it simply the experiences he's endured?
But what if these experiences are undesirable?
Where does he get help?

Is he to be abandoned to the medical establishment or is there some fundamental unwritten law that he's missed out on?

This book is specifically written for men facing their nemesis.

David Zachary Smith reveals a very profound, life-changing guide to refocus your mind and take back control of your destiny.

INTRODUCTION

This book has been written for men in their forties and beyond who suddenly find themselves saying "**WTF**" far too often. The views here are NOT politically correct. Nor are they intended to be offensive.

This book exposes the secrets and confidential meetings derived from Men's Private Business. I've been allowed to share these experiences to serve the greater good. Originally intended for 'Men's Eyes Only' this information is now released to the public. If you are a woman, you could be offended by the material in this book. Having stated that, the initial feedback from women who have read the proofs suggests that there's something here for everyone. Please let me know.

I encourage your feedback through my website: davidzacharysmith.com
where you can email or link to my Facebook and YouTube pages.

Thank you.

This book is in two parts.

Part 1: SECRET MEN'S BUSINESS

An explanation of your current life situation and where it's heading.

The Secret is revealed.

Part 2: COMMON GROUND

A detailed nine-year history of an ongoing Private Men's Group.

David Zachary Smith

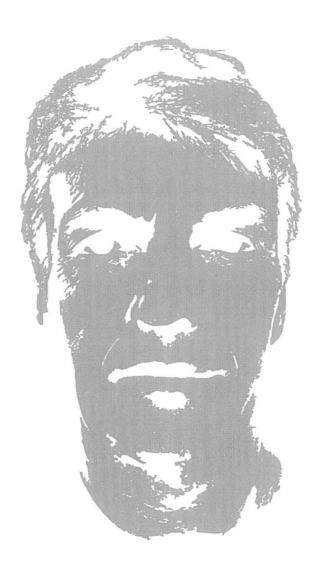

PREFACE

So, can I say, "Welcome to your middle age." A polite way of saying you are past it! You've ventured past the halfway point in your lifespan and everything you thought you knew has come into question.

Firstly, what is life all about?

Where is the enjoyment? Who is this person I married or have a relationship with? Why has everything gone sour? Why is there no sex? Why does PMT now last all month? Why are we arguing over basically nothing?

And Work Sucks!

You're stuck in a job you've been doing for too long or in a new job which is crap but you'll put up with it because you need the money.

There has to be some sort of logical explanation that deals with the life we men experience.

The new general term is being called manopause as opposed to women's menopause. Is it the change of life we men experience when we find our partner has already done so? Almost like a symptom but more likely a reaction? Or is it a change in our own right, a step into the next phase of our development?

There's a clever book written—*Men Are from Mars, Women Are from Venus*—which explains a lot. But let me give you the shortened version.

Women are just from a different planet, that's all you need to know. If you try to fathom the depths of the universe they exist in, then don your space suit and good luck!

Many a good man has gone before you and failed, but I urge you to read on before booking that rocket.

The change in men is from a very deep level, and unfortunately it will happen. Sooner rather than later your world will be turned upside down. You'll be hit by something that you didn't see coming.

Or let me paraphrase: You'll be hit by something you should've seen coming but your awareness level was quite subdued.

BUT! If your life is actually quite good and nothing written here has struck a chord, then do someone else a favour.

Give this book to a mate right now.

SECRET MEN'S BUSINESS

FEELINGS

Okay, so you are now middle-aged. Probably are in a marriage/defacto relationship with kids in their teens or older. Half of your mates have split with their wives/ partners. And each time you go to the beach you see more and more old guys running around with Asian girls who look no older than your daughter.

WTF is going on?

Not only that but you are now getting these strange feelings. You seem to have more empathy with the creatures around you. Your ego has softened somewhat and been replaced with a metaphysical sponge that is trying to relate to other people's problems.

How do you know this is happening? Because you seem to have very good advice for your mates who are in the same situation but bugger all aptitude to sort out your own bloody mess!

And your mess is getting messier ... The longer you delay your fate the more the **clouds of doom** descend until you're surrounded in so much fog that you can't see clearly from one day to the next!

The hardest part is trying to decipher what is the actual reality of your situation. An unbiased counsellor can be very helpful. The counsellor's recommendation then needs action and that is the painful part. But just realise this: if you can handle another five years of this torture then good luck to you. A martyrdom medal is on its way. Made of solid plastic, you can treasure it and pass it onto your grandkids!

WOMEN

Many years ago in the early sixties I received my first insight into women. This was the statement:

Women think with their heart; men think with their head.

I got that insight from an old family friend, Arthur Jones. I remember he had one of the first Holdens (Australian motor car) I had ever seen. An old FJ. Well, it was nearly new back then. I got to start and steer it along an old back road. Quite exciting stuff for a child whose family didn't have a car. And would you believe it had a starter button? Something that has now been reintroduced into the motorcar industry in the last few years.

I still remember that phrase today, obviously, otherwise I wouldn't have written it. But it is quite true. A woman's thoughts basically are charged with emotion. Men's generally aren't. So what the man thinks is how to logically look at a situation. A woman tries to get you to look at it from her point of view coupled with an emotion she is currently charged up with.

As I've explained with my book *SCI,* this states that neither are right, as there is no way of viewing the actual truth. Just one man or woman's observation of it at that time and place, plus the particular dimension their brain is operating in.

But this is **Secret Men's Business (SMB)**. And as such I am not trying to write to please everyone.

I am writing man to man.

David Zachary Smith

DIVORCE

Gather round, let me explain
There is a solution to all this pain
You already know it deep in your heart
It's pushing through you just like a fart

The person you loved has left long ago
The façade you see is only a glow
She left through her mind
Like a door was left open
Don't blame her ego
It knows nothing is broken

A hormonal change called the menopause
Blocked all her loving, closed all her doors
Don't ask her why, it's too hard to explain
Just realise this, she's swamped by the pain

So what do you do now
Inundated by conflicting reports
The counselling isn't working
Expensive lawyers are circling
Start submitting evidence to the courts
Welcome, my brother, to your Divorce!

This is a **Biggy**. This is what 50% of you reading this will experience in your lifetime.

Want to really know the woman you married or have a defacto relationship with? Then divorce her. I'm only saying this as a last resort, if all other avenues have been scanned, deliberated and scraped clean, so to speak. There's an old saying: 'Hell hath no fury like a woman scorned'. Most cases of divorce don't end well. What I mean is, all the faults that you have been accused of all your married/partnered life have now accumulated as a wall of treason to which you will pay **dearly**.

Fifty percent of you will go to court. Of that 50% half will actually proceed with the case in front of a judge. An agreement can be reached at the court steps, which means that the judge will help mediate your problems and tell you how much agony you will go through if you proceed. This usually helps stir the pot enough to get a result.

The Result

I'm constantly amazed at the men who find themselves in this situation who think that the financial split will be 50/50. Even without kids involved you will be very lucky with that outcome. With kids involved and you share their upbringing you will be really lucky to get 60/40 in her favour. Even if you have been the breadwinner and come into the relationship with all the money don't put a bet on anything better than retaining 40%. Why is this so? (Echoes of Julius Sumner Miller). It is so because our system of laws and courtroom procedure are geared towards the female who bears the children. Just ask any honest lawyer (joke?) and they'll tell you.

Once you set down the path of divorce then your new EX will focus on all the damage you have 'supposedly' done to her. And you will be the same, coupled with all your friends giving recommendations on both sides. Gradually you'll discover that some friends have alienated you because of stories, whether true or false, that have been said to them.

You'll try to keep your children separate from the entire goings-on, but they will either get exposed to it via friends of your EX or by direct communication. Either way they'll end up as a battering ram used by either party when the going gets heavy.

So you are BUGGERED whichever way you turn. So why do I say 'Want to really know the woman you married or long-time defacto partner?' Because you will release your ego and hers and they will battle to the end. It will probably get very bitter and very nasty and this is the root of ego. If you can both step aside from your egos and look at the bigger picture, then you will be part of a limited minority who actually have a successful separation.

Good luck!

WORK

Another inescapable fact of life. Work is unfortunately a necessity to pay for what we consume. It's actually a universal law, a cycle of life, if you prefer. But we humans have bastardised it to an extent that bugger all of us actually enjoy it.

The fact is that **WORK** in the western world is a four-letter word. To be associated with FUCK, SHIT, CRAP, PISS and any other expletive that evokes a feeling of rage or disgust!

Some men actually enjoy their work. They love working towards a goal and being paid for it. This is almost the Holy Grail of your

13

existence. If you truly enjoy your work, which in most cases takes a minimum of eight hours per day, then that is one third of your life that is worthwhile.

For those who do not enjoy their work then be warned! There is a **Silent Partner (SP)** in your subconsciousness that will actually go on the attack, and subsequently make these eight hours much worse for you. You will recognise this since you're getting sick more than usual. The occasional workplace accident will start being quite frequent. You'll suffer injuries to your muscles, tendons, joints, etc. whether you're at work or not. These manifest to get you to quit what you hate doing. The more actual time you spend doing what you dislike the worse it will get.

For example, I was working in a bus company that was very badly run by the owners. As a mechanic I was responsible to repair and maintain a fleet of tourist buses that were on the road right around the clock. When my apprentices and I finally got a chance to repair the buses they were usually completely unserviceable; in other words, worn out! So we were always under the gun and had many a rush job so a tour could get out on time.

I hated the job but considered there was nothing else available. I also had a baby on the way with my partner who was working in a job that she didn't like either. I felt enormous pressure from the occupation I disliked and the impending responsibility of a new family member.

One morning I had a new apprentice help me with a 4WD bus that needed its front brake shoes replaced and a broken reversing light globe changed. I jacked up the front wheels, put axle stands under the differential housing and pulled off the passenger side wheel. The rear wheels were left on the ground. I then positioned my body underneath the front axle checking the oil level. My apprentice meanwhile was working at the back taking the light globe out. I knew this as I could see where his feet were positioned.

Next thing, he walked around to the front of the vehicle and jumped into the driver's seat. He started the engine, pushed in the clutch pedal and immediately selected reverse gear (I could hear the box grind as he pulled the gear stick). I remember yelling, "What are you bloody doing?" Then he released the clutch and the whole truck lurched off the axle stand and fell straight down on top of my legs and lower back, slamming me into the concrete floor.

An extremely painful experience and a quick trip in the ambulance and three years of rehab later I was back to work. Not the same job but one much more pleasant.

The point being that now in hindsight I can realise what happened. This has also been experienced by many of my friends, some of which have been years at an occupation they intensely dislike. Now they're paying the price, with injury-related workers' compensation, stress leave or constant bouts of sickness and migraines, etc. Anything that you intensely dislike will invoke your **SP**. Your Silent Partner will try to alleviate you of that situation by preventing you from doing it. This will be explained in more detail later. But know this: If you work in a place that you intensely dislike then you'll certainly get to your grave much faster.

DIET

So you want to lose weight? Let me guess why. After ogling at boobs half your life you're now sporting a sizeable set yourself! Plus, your gut looks like Arnold Schwarzenegger's six-pack from 1994 ... in the movie *Junior*!

So what choices do you have? Diet, exercise or medical intervention?

There are so many different diets these days: Paleo, Pritikin, vegan, vegetarian, DASH, MIND, Weight Watchers, cabbage diet, liquid-only diet, and recently the protein-only diet.

Also many various ways to put your body through torture: gym, boot camp, saunas, boxercise. Then there's the metaphysical, meditation, hypnosis, shock therapy, etc.

You can also have gastric intervention by having surgery to fit a band around your stomach.

Then if that isn't enough, there are these bloody exercise machines on every second advert on TV. Each new one finds an area of the body that the last one missed and they convince you that this one is the holy grail.

Let me help you. There is one overriding factor that you cannot avoid if you want to lose weight! That is, we in the Western world EAT TOO MUCH. And the cure is … wait for it! DON'T EAT.

Am I fair dinkum? YES! I do this and have done so regularly when I think I've had enough.

If you haven't got the willpower to eat bugger all until you lose all that fat, then don't bother going on a fad diet. I'll save you all that money by saying, "All that fat will return".

DEPRESSION

I looked outside to find the blame
I looked inside and found my name.

Depression is another experience lurking in the shadows of your mind. But you can be one of the lucky ones and miss it altogether, depending on life experience, personality and your personal mind filter. Depression is the mind in regression, basically looking back. The difficulty is that the focus is mostly on all the problems in your life. Notice I said problems, not challenges. A challenge is something you take on willingly and many people now use that word as a replacement for problem. A problem is something that you are presented with and it's up to you to fix it, even though you would largely prefer not to.

A real bout of sustained depression is usually brought on by a number of hits. For a male it usually culminates at age 40+ combined with a mid-life crisis. Deep-seated questions about life coupled with an impending divorce/ separation, career change, weight gain and lack of or rejection of intimacy.

The mind then takes over with constant talk in a derogatory manner. This 'talker' eventually takes on its own identity and subsequently hammers you day and night, belittling your mind to the point of no return. To gain a rough insight here is a poem that I constructed around the days at my lowest ebb whereby taking my life seemed the only option out.

Passing Time Till I Die

The life in your head is stricken with remorse
No relief in sight to alter its course
The depth of depression
Its lead straps that bind you
Get back on the horse I'm here to remind you
But the horse is broken and I cannot see
Is this the chance that life is offering me?

To walk the path of mediocre soil
Abandoning hope to a life of toil
With this my last breath I let out a sigh
How pointless this life
Passing time till I die.

Not only was my mind immersed in depression 'looking back', it also copped anxiety 'looking forward'. So with the double whammy of a depressed past and no future you can see the inevitable result.

As I write this, on this day Robin Williams, the world-renowned comedian/actor, has taken his own life. And unfortunately so have many others before him, in and out of the public eye.

After my 'event', as I call it, I struggled to exist for many months. The identity in my head had a metaphysical form at that time. Picture a scene in a coffee shop. I'm at one table and this metaphysical form, a body double, is sitting at a table not far away. I feel his intense stare strongly as he studies me for any sign of defeat. He just waits for a chance to walk back in and destroy me. At times he'll push his chair back and half stand when he can see me weakening. Any thoughts of remorse or sickening anxiety are his fuel. That's the signal to come back in and take me down.

As a man who has been to the brink, I know what it is to face my own demons. For me the voice in my head just kept reminding me of everything that had gone wrong in my life. Every waking moment it'd be reminding me of what a totally useless being I was and my future prospects in life were just zero. Actually I couldn't see a future at all. I had no self-esteem whatsoever.

Sleep was my only saviour; I spent many days in bed. If I was awake I'd be curled up (foetal position) on the kitchen floor asking for something to help me end it all.

What saved me? I learned the **Secret.** Then discovered my **Silent Partner (SP)** was on the attack. People I'd opened up to about my problem tried to help too but I realised that my own extremely negative thoughts fed by my ego were my worst enemy. Every day I had to literally kick them out of my head.

As for the suicide tendencies I eventually understood that death was inevitable, there's no bonus in getting there faster. The entity is still there though, in the back of my mind.

Depression is a mental virus; you can't delete a virus from your system. I liken it to a bad twin or spirit who's just waiting for an opportunity to retake my soul, and remind me of how worthless I am. But as I say, everything turned around.

HELP

Some people don't want help!

Having tried to help men with their recurring depressive thoughts I have come across this situation a few times. Their depressive story is such a part of their personality they can't divorce it. It's killing them, mind you, but there is no comprehension of this. To release the story is to cut off a limb. This limb is impossible to function without. So they go on, and on, and on with that depressing scenario of what was done to them by another uncaring person.

How do you recognise someone like this? It's easy: ask them about what has happened or what makes them sad and they can actually give you dates and times of every situation that materialised in their past.

Plus, actually quote other people word for word as to what was said. Essentially every time you see them, same story, same quotes, same ending. They'll be triggered by anything you say that reminds them of their own situation. And then you have to listen to that same story unfold with all the details again, and again, and again.

Why are they like this? Their 'story' of sadness exists in their mind; it's locked in. It reminds them every waking hour of what happened and will pervade their thoughts, especially when all else is quiet. It is such a part of them that it's their truth, it's who they are, and you won't change that.

YOUR FUTURE

Let me predict your future. It may surprise you that you will get exactly what everyone else gets. Rich or poor, young or old, adored by millions or only known by a few. Let me save you the time perusing over many books and documents to the wee hours searching for life's secret!

Don't bother going to palm readers or fortune tellers either. I'm about to save you tons of money.

The fact is quite overwhelming. Prepare yourself because this is going to be quite confronting!

You're going to DIE!

Yes, that's right, and you can pass that on to whomever you like and I won't require any royalties from you either. Yes, dear reader, death is inevitable. So why are you here at all? What is the point of your existence?

It's simply for the experience of life itself.

And by reading this book you'll learn a way to enhance your experience.

WTF

You know, back in 2013 I was literally saying to myself, "What the fuck". I recall this phrase having been uttered by Jesse Ventura in the movie *Predator*, one of my favourites; well, anything with Arnold Schwarzenegger is a favourite. He stated "What the fuck" when first catching sight of the alien (Predator), overwhelmed/awestruck by its existence.

But I'm not stating WTF as being awestruck or being overwhelmed. I'm stating it relating to the fact that at that time I'd just given up. Not in the sense of relinquishing my grip on existence itself, but just that my life course had been set and try as I might I couldn't change it.

For example, trying to avoid situations and circumstances with past relationships had only really paused me for a time and then chucked me right back into it. I blame the 'law of attraction', which will be explained later, for my situation. Well, I have to blame something. Notice I have not blamed 'someone'; that subject will also be covered later. As the law of attraction is in itself part of my existence then I am saying "I Blame Myself".

Blaming yourself is actually quite rewarding. Have you ever tried it? You just chant to yourself "I'm a fucken stupid idiot" over a number of hours until you actually believe it. That's when you get to what I call a 'Base Level' of self-understanding. From there you can actually see the game you have been playing with yourself, with your life. And you finally can come to a realisation that no matter what you have done, or will do, you will mentally arrive at this exact point in your life. That is Inevitability!

Notice I said exact 'mental' point, not financial or any other type of assumed status.

I'm talking about the actual person you have believed you are and formed a mental opinion of. All people from all walks of life are subject to this, no more apparent than when you see a news report of a rich and famous member of the Facebook elite or any other self-possessed person of the supposed privileged in society taking their own life. You can hear people say, "But he/she had everything: fame, fortune, a beautiful wife or handsome husband, a fantastic palace in the Bahamas; how on earth did that happen?"

It's easy, they just had mind talk that really wasn't beneficial to their existence and had no ability to realise this. This talk invokes their **Silent Partner (SP)**; once involved it's all downhill from there on.

And if you can actually see this 'talk' clearly you then have the ability to step outside of your vessel, your human body, and become the puppeteer; that is, to pull the strings at the right time and place so the puppet (you) can interact with all the other puppets who haven't any idea that they're trapped in their own confusing dimensions as well.

You actually can disassociate yourself from the human game. And make no mistake, it is a game like any other: monopoly, chess or checkers. There is no real rational truth to life and only one way out of it once you're in.

This might actually portray to you that I'm a bit of a sad sack. Not at all, I'm in it for the experience; there is really nothing more basic than that.

So WTF, my friends, it doesn't matter, truly. It may surprise you that there are many times that you don't actually exist. Yes, that's right! If someone is not thinking about you or observing you then you actually don't exist to them. You only really exist in yourself, your particular dimension, your mind-set. And that is only at this brief moment in time. So you can just say to yourself WTF and be done with it. Now start pulling the strings.

So WTF am I trying to say here? Well, basically, if you are in a relationship that you dislike intensely then leave. That is part of your experience. But I warn you, if you enter into another relationship you will sooner or later find yourself back in the same situation. Welcome to the law of attraction.

LAW OF ATTRACTION

GT Capri

Many years ago in the 80s I had my first experience of the law of attraction. Of course I didn't know there was such a thing back then but I was in awe of the experience. In those days my mates and I loved cars and couldn't wait to have one of our own. One of my friends who left school much earlier than the rest of us bought himself a 1971 model Ford Capri GT V6, red with black GT stripes. Beautiful car. Quite rare back then to see any on the road. He had a relationship with his girlfriend that lasted a few years. Considering he was only about 18 it was quite an achievement back then.

One day though there were problems afoot and they parted company. He was quite upset and talked to me about the situation but refrained from elaborating to anyone else.

I remember months later being at a party with him and some other mates and the subject came up about his relationship. He 'fessed up that it was over some months back to the astonishment of the others. They were not astonished by the fact that they had broken up, just that they didn't believe him and told him as much. The fact being that many people had seen his car with him and his girlfriend driving around in it. Can't mistake the car: Ford Capri GT V6 red with black GT stripes. And can't mistake him with his dark features and his girlfriend's frizzy hair.

He answered their objections by asking, "Did you look at the wheels?" The guys who were, shall we say, Car Mad, as most blokes were back then, answered, "Yeah, chrome 12 slotters, did you update them?" "No," he answered. And we all went outside to look at his car again with its unusual alloy wheels.

That event stuck in my mind as the first ever experience I had seen of the law of attraction. My friend's replacement not only looked like him but his car (being quite rare) was the same model, year, paint, right down to the wheels which were all chrome instead of alloy. I remember pondering to myself at that time, how could this be a coincidence?

But now of course after much more experience I see this all the time. In myself as well as others. And I can see why men and women have multiple marriages. They end up quite dissatisfied with their partner after they eventually find out they've basically married the same person in a different skin.

Now I'm not saying that is bad. A puppet doesn't know it's being manipulated. If you realise the game, then you know the inevitability of it all. What you need to know is you don't have to continue being a puppet, you can be the puppeteer. How do you become this? You get in touch with your **Silent Partner (SP).** If you continue being the puppet, then you'll miss out on a very important aspect of your life. To take back control of your own destiny.

So who is this **SP**?

UNIVERSE/MULTIVERSE QUANTUM THEORY

There is a suggestion that there seems to be more to our life than just the universe we exist in. In fact, many universes exist in multiple different dimensions. I'll dare to take that one step further by saying that we each exist in our own universe, each one different from the next. In effect, 6.5 billion universes exist in the minds of people on this planet. Each person's mind creating its own set of circumstances to enable it to see its existence. No one the same but many similar.

To take another step then we are in fact our own Gods of our own universe that exist in the consciousness of all beings on this planet. Even each experience we have is filtered by our mind screen which then alters the individual experience. That's why in a court room you can have many witnesses who saw the same event but a good lawyer will pick holes in each person's statement because they aren't aware of the differences between them. You can get close to the truth and reality but as we are human we'll never experience it until all the mind 'garbage' has been scraped away.

For example, look at a simple object that is, say, less than three metres away. Do you see the actual truth of that image? If you viewed it from the side or behind would it look different? Can you see anything between you and this image? Do you see the millions of atoms of oxygen and nitrogen in the air between you and it? Do you realise it is in fact vibrating as we all are? Can you see the porous nature of this thing? Do you realise that like everything else it's made up of mostly air?

So what does this mean for us, day to day?

It means that we are not really aware of our connection through consciousness with our existence. And to be more aware we must find a connection to communicate with consciousness. And the way to connect is through spirit.

SPIRIT

There are many books now on spiritual concepts. And most of these dance around very important lessons for us physically bound souls. I have had very personal experience with this during my manopause and I can tell you if you actually touch this part of you, the real essence of who you are, it is the most beautiful realisation you will ever have. To find your spirit which totally envelops you in love and to know that it alone will never leave your side no matter what is the most encouraging feeling you will ever experience.

I'm not talking about God or some type of religious experience. Because they are all fallible. Why is that? The simple fact is they are man-made. As soon as another human states stuff about a God and how he has made all these laws, etc. alarm bells should start ringing.

Also if someone declares they are God's representative as they have studied a religion or have meditated for 20 years and are somehow above us all then that alarm should be restarted. Fact is no-one is above you or anything else in the hierarchy of things on this planet or anywhere else in the universe.

We are no worthier than a rat, spider or monkey, or the rock you are sitting on, and vice versa. Even a virus or any other compilation of atoms that exist in this moment of time that we all exist in is no worthier than any other. If you think you are great, then that is good for your self-esteem and I commend you. But don't expect a medal to declare that you are any greater than the dirt you are presently standing on!

Let me explain spirit. By spirit I mean the actual non-physical you. The physical you is your actual body and its current experience of your existence. The non-physical you is your core essence. Best explained by your thoughts. If you think of something, say, an apple, you can see the apple in your mind but it has no physical reality. Your thoughts have no physical structure yet they pour through your mind constantly. Your spirit is much like your thoughts. It's a duplicate of you in the non-physical dimension. It exists in a dimension not bound by human laws. There are no good or bad, right or wrong, or any other restrictions. It's just there to help you. Whichever way you want your direction in life to take it'll be with you 100%. No exceptions!

Religion usually has a god at the helm and there are all sorts of rules and regulations to follow. These will be provided by a bible of some sort which has been rewritten and misinterpreted over the centuries to a point whereby it currently confuses most educated people who have had any dealings with it. Most religions will scare you by saying that there's a bloke on the other side counting up all your sins and you're about to be punished for all eternity when you're dead. But that doesn't really help all those people currently being slaughtered by a self-appointed dictator, does it?

It's quite typical to hear someone ask why God would allow such tragedies to befall upon man. Most religious organisations have a response that "it's for the higher good of which we quite don't understand" … You can ask, why would God allow a paedophile to interfere with a young child? And you'd get an underhanded answer: "To allow this child to help others who have also had this experience" or "The love of God will enter the child to forgive the perpetrator". But does that also work when the paedophile is a priest, ordained by the church, sanctioned by God?

Another classic example is the aftermath of 9/11. People were asking where God was when all those people died inside the twin towers. I remember seeing answers like "God sent the firemen inside to rescue them" … But didn't they get killed too? You can see if you ever question someone's belief in their God then you join their merry-go-round of illusion.

Spirit is quite separate to God. Spirit will help whichever way you turn. If you want to love or hate it'll be there 100 %. That is why the assassins flying the planes on 9/11 did what they planned to do without God intervening. That is why Adolf Hitler and a host of other dictators can do exactly what they want to do without answering to God.

People have used the power of God to do a lot of good in this world too, don't get me wrong there. But the God they think they're using is actually the spirit inside that is with them all the way. This happens to so-called 'holy people' as well …

There seems to be an aura around them that attracts followers. The love of their consciousness envelops many people and things. This then leads us to our **Silent Partner.** Have you figured out who it is?

Once you have connection with your spirit you'll never be lonely or alone again.

It is basically one of the most important discoveries you'll ever experience. This happens to a great many people; however, it gets bastardised by attaching this enlightenment to a religious organisation.

SPIRIT, SILENT PARTNER (SP)

I have to also elaborate on my statement.

Once you have connection with your spirit you'll never be lonely or alone again. You are actually connected with your spirit whether you like it or not. It's part of you and is always acting on your behalf.

If you think about the movie *Avatar* it's almost the same concept: two bodies run by one consciousness. The main character, Jake Sully, enters the other body (Avatar) through his subconscious.

The spirit I refer to is your link to consciousness. I call it 'silent' as it's constantly working in the background.

The 'connection' I'm talking about is to actually converse with it. It's not as easy as picking up the phone but a regular hook-up is actually quite beneficial to your wellbeing. You will need to quieten down your mind talk, your thinking, as this tends to fill up the space you need for communication. If you let go of all the constant mind talk and rubbish about the past and the possible future which invades your headspace constantly then that gap will be filled by this 'spirit'.

The more times you let it in the better life gets. How do you do this? Just read on!

David Zachary Smith

THE SECRET

In honour of my mentor RT

I weep for the men of this world
*For they know not the **Secret***
Deceased but still breathing
Existing in the shallowest of graves
Gasping for recognition
Devoid of connection
A dimension of their own manifestation

These are the four paramount ways to connect with spirit and consciousness.

1. Sense drop
2. Breathing
3. Toning
4. Automatic writing

All but automatic writing can be done singularly or in a group. A group can help initially as the leader can call the times and instruct on the focus points. Let's start with:

1. SENSE DROP

Sight, sound, feel and drop. The first three words refer to three basic senses. The last word is a mind visualisation.

So firstly you will need to get yourself in a quiet room, preferably first up in the morning. Sit down, get comfortable and make sure you're not disturbed for 10 minutes.

SIGHT

Now, just look at something. It could be a picture on the far wall or a book on a coffee table. Now within this vision try to concentrate on a very small part of it. If the picture is of a car, for example, just focus your eyes on one wheel. If you're looking at a book on the coffee table just look at one letter. Now focus on this one small part. Recognise its colour, look at how it differentiates itself from the background. Let go of your mind trying to give it a name, just look at it from a pure existence level. Focus your whole mind on this for approximately one minute.

SOUND

Now close your eyes. Listen to the noises around you; you may be in a quiet place but can you hear the wind? A bird chirping in the distance. A clock ticking off the seconds. Listen intently. This should last another minute.

FEEL

Now, still seated with eyes closed, try feeling the presence of your hands. Don't touch them together as you need to be quite still. Normally focusing on your hands will result in a tingling sensation. If you can't feel this, then focus on what your hands are resting on. The pressure from the weight of your hand against the seat. Now the same with your back. Feel its pressure against your seat. Feel the temperature difference. Now feel the seat on your backside. Feel all the weight of your body there. Feel the material against your skin. Now move to your legs and feet. Feel them resting against the floor. Note the pressure and temperature difference. Do this for about one minute.

DROP

Now you need to create a picture in your mind. See yourself floating on the surface of an ocean. Nothing between you and the horizon as far as you can see. Totally relax there. There are no waves and nothing of any importance around. Now you are starting to submerge. Encapsulated in a bubble, you have no trouble breathing. You are floating down, down, down. Till all you can see is a tiny light way up on the surface. Keep going down and now that light fades from view. Now totally dark you are on the bottom of the ocean. It is totally inky black all around you. Settle there. You are all alone. Nothing to trouble you. Nothing else in existence. Stay there for one minute. Now you feel a gentle bump and you've started floating again. A small dot of light way up in the distance grows ever wider and brighter. Still floating you are halfway. Now you are seeing a wide expanse of blue through the water. The light is penetrating all around you. Now you break through the surface. OPEN YOUR EYES.

You need to practise this for around seven days before you get to the next level.

2. BREATHING

Breath or breathing is one of the most basic forms of meditation. Once mastered you can practise this anywhere, which, as you will understand, is very handy. Everyone breathes; of course, it's a basic form of existence. But what I'm talking about here is the focus on breathing. If you focus on your breathing, then this tends to shut other things out of your mind.

Firstly, close your eyes. That's one stimulus that we can shut out right there. So let's start with the breath in. Draw air into your lungs quite deeply. As you do this feel your chest cavity expand. Feel the stretching. Notice the air as it flows past your lips. Hear the noise it makes against your teeth as it pours in. Now let the air out slowly. Feel the shrinkage in your body as it escapes. Feel the warmth of the now body-heated air escaping through your mouth. Listen to the noise it makes. Now breathe in again, deeply. Feel and listen to the difference in your body. Now breathe out again. Focus on any differences you feel each time you do this. Breathe in, breathe out. Do this for about five minutes.

As with sense drop you will need to do this first up every morning for seven days to get in practice. Alternate with sense drop and breathing to get your mind used to the practice. The breathing method works very well. I have found it's a great backup. It can work in places where you are stuck. For example, in a line waiting for tickets. The line is a mile long and you will come to no harm if you switch off for a few minutes or even seconds. You will be able to feel or hear if the line starts moving again. But the connecting with consciousness will be well worth it.

It helps to clarify what is around you. Your intuition level will pick up a great deal too. The more you do this the greater the connection. Some people get lost in it. Gurus get lost in it. It's a very pleasant place to exist. Just be careful though. You can end up being there more often than not and become completely disconnected with the real world. That is not advisable. This is a method of help and direction. Not a destination!

Breathing is the quick connect. Sense drop is the ritual. Mastering the sense drop is paramount. Once mastered you will find many things alter in your consciousness.

Your intuition ability will literally go through the roof! And you'll be able to interact with the conscious connection that envelops all humanity. The life you live which you perhaps thought was a series of random events will now have a new player at the controls. And that new player is YOU!

CONTROLLING DESTINY

Here's the exciting bit. Once you have nailed the sense drop you will find yourself just slipping into the drop part more easily. Finding peace in the darkness. Floating back into the light will be more rapid too. When you open your eyes, that's the point when you start the conversation. For example, if you are trying to figure out a way to fix an item or if you're working on something that just isn't quite up to scratch, ask for help. You can ask in your mind or verbally if you like. Just say, for example, "I need to see what is missing with this—name the problem—so I can complete it." It especially works well if you are inventing something that isn't on anyone's radar at the moment. You can ask to be shown any new ideas or new types of angles to look at the invention.

This is nothing new to the uninitiated. Let's use an example: I find transport the easiest because most people are involved with it on a daily basis. Say a friend wants to buy a car. He explains the make and model and you say, "Well, I haven't seen any about, are you sure it's a good idea?" He tells you about it and sends you a link via email to check out a picture online. After seeing this the next day, you drive to work and you see one, then another, then perhaps even more.

How can that be? Even if it's a fairly rare car you will see one somewhere. The answer is it has entered your consciousness. Now it exists. Before it didn't exist in your mind so you didn't recognise it. You probably drove past one every day but there was no recognition on your behalf. Consciousness doesn't bring the car into existence, it just allows you to recognise it exists.

The **sense drop** allows you to actually converse with spirit through consciousness to create a link to existence. It doesn't magically create what you want, but leads you to a conversation, situation or place whereby you will witness what you need.

SD allows direct influence over consciousness by breaking down the barriers and hastening the steps towards the goal. It gets you there much quicker by showing you the pathway.

So what about **breathing**?

Breathing just gets your mind centred. Like having a shower after a long, hard day's work. It is the relief from all your mind babble. The act of breathing control has a direct link with intuition. Previous incidences of this type of instinctiveness will now almost become commonplace. You will literally feel what others feel. You will know the ending of a book even before halfway through. You will know the winner of a competition on television way before it's announced. You will know when you're near someone who is anxious or depressed even though they have no outward signs of this.

The more you are at ease with this the more you will understand people and situations without actually having conscious reasoning behind your evaluation.

Here are some examples of early personal experiences with my new link to consciousness.

THE INVENTION

At one stage after a sense drop I asked about an invention I had been toying around with in my head. I wanted to get more leverage from a standard pedalling system on a bicycle.

A standard bicycle crank is 6 ½ inches or 175mm long. That gives it a leverage advantage so the effort to pedal the bike is multiplied. Did you ever ride one of the old dragsters from the 70s? Great on the flat but once you have to climb a hill they're absolute torture. Their crank levers are shorter thus their leverage advantage is greatly reduced. What I wanted was a crank lever two to three times the size. But that was not practical. Increasing the length of the standard bicycle crank would mean you'd hit the pavement on the downstroke going around corners. Also your knee would be uncomfortably high on the upstroke.

This was my dilemma. So late one evening, just before bed, I decided to perform an SD, asking for a solution. I would normally do this in the morning so for me it was a new experience. That night I actually dreamt that I was riding the new bicycle. I awakened at 2 a.m. with so much excitement that I searched for paper and pen to draw a picture of it. It had long levers attached to a pivot point on the frame above the crank sprocket. Small levers then connected to the original crank. The large levers just went up and down; gone was the rotary motion of your legs. It looked a little like the old steam-train wheels connected by the rod and pin. This turned the reciprocating motion into rotary motion. Much like a crankshaft and conrod in a combustion engine.

Sleep now was not an option; the fact is, I was so excited that I couldn't sleep. In hindsight this would've been more appropriate in daylight. So keep the SD as a morning ritual: be warned!

With picture in hand, proceeding out into the garage I started building a working model to see if it would function correctly. To my surprise it did! Then over the next few weeks I had a local engineering firm make the parts needed to attach to a bike I modified.

So what happened to the bicycle invention? Well, I actually made the bike and rode it around for a while. It worked and had more leverage than any other bike out there, but lost most of that advantage because of all the extra moving parts. The standard bicycle system is hard to beat because of its function and simplicity. I'm, however, very satisfied with my invention. I may someday actually develop what I've named the 'Dreamlever' too.

BEN

Every spirit has its own name. So how do you find out? Just ask. But it doesn't just reply in the normal sense. A conversation with your spirit is more cryptic than that. When I asked mine it implied, "You have always known my name." (Okay, strap yourselves in, childhood memory exposure coming up). The only name in memory was my invisible friend named Ben who I had a special relationship with when I was very young. He lived in a bush halfway down the garden path and I'd go there every day on my own to catch up. I had a brief second guess with myself: can this really be the right name? Then I experienced an emotional connection to that name but before now never consciously realised it.

Michael Jackson sung the song 'Ben' for the 1972 film of the same name. Every time I have ever heard that song it brought me to tears. If in the presence of other people and it popped up on the radio I would have to excuse myself so my friends didn't think Dave was looney. I now realise why. The song is about a powerful friendship that can't be broken. Once I realised all of this, BEN has been the catalyst for me. When the name presents itself I always take special notice.

So it was midway into 2015 and I decided to try my hand in the Australian stock market. Which for most people means that you're going to throw half your money away in the short term or wait three years for it to come off its lows so you can get your money back.

A friend recently contacted me and said that Bendigo Bank was looking cheap and was coming up for a good dividend soon. Its stock symbol is BEN. There's the connection, I immediately thought. I had a bit of spare money at that time and bought 2500 shares. Three days later, before its dividend announcement date, its price plummeted. Down 50c; I was shocked. How could a bank drop so much? Why would people dump it before you receive your dividend? Anyway, my instinct told me to hold on. Three weeks later I had made $1200 and was due $1000 dividend in the bank a month after that. I just then traded in and out of BEN. When the price dropped down enough that signalled a buy. When the price shot up I would sell.

I averaged over $600 per week for the next six months until my spirit said time to pull out. Now, it's not a fortune. But a weekly wage for just watching one stock. A stock that had been shown to me with its obvious connection.

Now you can say, and rightly so, that bank stocks are relatively easy to make money on and in the scheme of things I wouldn't argue. But at one time BEN's price was fairly high for about three weeks and the general market was looking good. So I decided to buy back, thinking that a new level high was imminent. So one morning as the market opened I bought in. Within 10 minutes the stock started falling. As always my eyes were on the other bank stocks and the market in general but they were edging higher. For some unknown reason someone was dumping large amounts of stock and within 20 minutes I was $200 down. Then $250, $300, $350; every five minutes down it went. So I sold out. Doing my calculations at the end of the day I noticed that when I dumped there was a small bounce and luckily my loss was only $250.

But here's the weird thing. Once the transaction finally made it into my account I was $200 up! Yes, that's right! Instead of $250 down it was $200 up. Even the online trader couldn't explain it.

The only way I can explain this is as I've said before. Your spirit backs you all the way, no question. So, ask for a name, then you'll become aware that that very name has been presenting itself to you all your life. This name will be very important, so take notice.

BREXIT

Anyone who plays the stock market knows there is no better time to buy stocks than when everyone has sold out and prices are unrealistically low. So when major world events take centre stage you need to be ready. I had a premonition about Brexit, believing that it would be a close call but ultimately Britain would leave the EU. I specifically remember the day of the announcement.

I was having coffee at a local shop while checking the Australian market on my phone app. Then switching from the market app to news updates and back again. There was a false call that stated they would stay and the market surged up. I instinctively knew this was wrong and waited. Then came the update that they would exit. Market panic followed and stocks were diving everywhere. I spent that afternoon buying all my favourite stocks and really made good money selling them about one month later.

TRUMP

Six months before the US election I knew Donald Trump would be elected president.

How did I know this? I didn't. But consciousness did. At that time most of my friends were saying that my prediction was preposterous. "Why on earth would the American people vote him in?" But I stood my ground. Realising the worldwide implications, I also prepared myself for the stock market, making sure that I had cashed in all my stocks a month before the election, thereby allowing plenty of unencumbered money to spend.

So on the day, as with Brexit, there was an early false call. The news announced Clinton would win. The market surged but I held back. Then of course as we all know the news reversed its decision. There was a subsequent huge dump on the Australian stock market. So much so that near the end of trading where I believed it had bottomed there were huge numbers of traders with the same belief.

The whole system jammed up. Not only that but the telecom supplier I used also slowed to a halt. So only half my trades went through.

But luckily the next day it was still down so I completed them. And rode the wave of buying till I had made good money again.

MELBOURNE CUP

With my newfound power I decided to try another experiment. Why not use the **SD** to find the winner of the Melbourne Cup? Back in 2014 I accurately predicted that Protectionist would win. I did this by having a list of the horses and jockeys from the local newspaper spread out in front of me. I performed an SD then opened my eyes and scanned the page. My eyesight was immediately drawn to that horse. I can't explain why but it was almost intuitive that he would win. So I put money on him and was very pleased with the result.

So come 2015 I decided to try again. Performing the same ritual and then scanning the field page I was immediately drawn to Prince of Penzance. Then, pleased with myself, I began reading the statistics. A female jockey and over 100/1 odds. Firstly, a female jockey has never won the Melbourne Cup. And only one other horse in history has won the cup at such long odds. So my ego kicked in and the next few hours were spent second guessing myself. By the time I put a bet on I was only prepared to risk $1 because the odds of that horse winning were too great and I'm sure I must've done the SD wrong or possibly hadn't cleared my mind properly. Prince of Penzance won!

LOTTERIES

At this stage I believe it's worth talking about gambling. Using the **SD** in the previous example is different to picking lotto numbers. If it was that easy then you wouldn't be reading this book and I'd be pictured waving on a postcard from the Bahamas.

Why? Because lotto numbers are a totally random occurrence. Horse racing, that is the horse's jockeys and everything else involved that is connected through consciousness. The SD shows the path, not actually the final destination. If, for example, you used the SD to bring money into your life you will be shown the path to do this. You may be drawn to place some money on lotto but the numbers used will be a problem. If, for example, the numbers had already been drawn, then those would have entered consciousness through people who had observed them. This would then allow you to access those numbers through a SD ritual. So a random sequence of numbers cannot be accessed by consciousness.

However, a 'lucky number' that has significance in your life can be accessed and will be presented to you at every opportunity.

GROCERIES

I decided on another experiment to double check the veracity of what I was experiencing. I had been given a grocery list to collect at the local shop. The shop was called Woolworths and every aisle had a list hanging above it stating what was there. I ignored the signs. What if it was still possible to find the groceries I needed? Could my spirit guide me right to each item?

Outside I did a brief SD and looked at the list. Then inside without looking up I slowly walked along the front access. Passing one particular aisle I felt this really warm, almost burning feeling. So I stopped, walked down it and continued till the sensation ceased. Then looking either side of me I would see the grocery I had pictured in my mind.

I did this for all the 12 items on the list. The sensation would disappear within a one-metre range; the feeling didn't run right up to the actual item. But I was amazed at how accurate this was.

ON THE ROAD

For seven years I worked as a courier delivering flowers. The last two of those years I was in the midst of this new discovery.

Once while on deliveries I had been following a slow car down a windy back road. The road was too dangerous to pass but as usual I was in a hurry. Frustrated, I followed for about a kilometre, then thought, why not ask my spirit to ask her spirit to pull over? I had no time to do the usual rituals so I just focused on the car. Almost immediately it pulled over and let me pass.

One day I stopped behind a car at a T-intersection. Nothing abnormal; that is, until I sat there for about a minute with no traffic coming either way. My intuition immediately told me that the driver was a female, out of fuel and she needed help. I put my hazard lights on and walked to her side window. She was busy cranking the engine over via the ignition key but nothing would fire up. "No fuel?" I asked. "Not sure," she replied. "Fuel gauge says empty but it's been broken for a month."

I was in a hurry for the next delivery so I asked her if she was in RACQ (a state-wide roadside assist company). She said "Yes." Then who should pull up behind me? An RACQ van. I motioned to the driver to help me push her to the side of the road. As he was doing this I told him she was a member. He helped her straight away. All the time this scenario was happening it had already played out in my mind. I instinctively knew what was wrong and that help was coming immediately.

With deliveries you often share the car parks at shop fronts (called loading zones) with other drivers. I knew instinctively that one man who I'd seen quite often was called Dave. There was no explanation or rational thought behind this, I just naturally thought it would be. So one day, I asked, "So how are you today, Dave?" He was a bit amazed as we had never spoken. Even more amazed that I knew his name. Sure enough, spirit was right again.

In the midst of my new discovery I decided on another experiment. I thought, is it possible to see the next house I'm delivering to even though I'd never been there before? So I pulled to the side of the road and did the sense drop.

Opening my eyes, I looked at the next address on my delivery sheet. Now, with my mind focused on the address, I shut my eyes to see its physical manifestation. A picture appeared, revealing the next house I was delivering to.

The picture was as though it was looking from the driveway. I could see the house number, letterbox, fence and brickwork. It was like I had travelled in time, witnessing what I was about to see half an hour later. All I had to do was look at the address. I tried this on many occasions to check and each time the result was the same. But I had to do it with a clear mind, early in the morning. After two apparitions my mind would start to second guess the result and that threw the predictions right out. So I would have to limit them to two only for accuracy.

NIGHT AND DAY

Why do I use **SD** in the morning? The only reason I do this is because once you ask spirit for guidance it does so as soon as possible. And will keep it up all day till you fall asleep again at night time. This ends the cycle. If you do this before you sleep then the info will be sent in a dream that will literally wake you up!

As in my **Invention** story. Then you will spend most of the night chasing up this information and you'll miss out on valuable sleep.

But if something has been troubling you and it has bothered you all day then it may be worth your while to do a SD before you go to bed. If you are troubled then most probably you won't get to sleep anyway, so you may as well get the answer. You can also use the SD to let you sleep until the answer is shown to you. I have an example of this.

GERBER SHEATH

I have a Gerber multi-tool. Having owned it for many years it rarely leaves my side. The Gerber usually sits inside a sheath attached to my belt. At night I take it off my belt, placing it on my bedside table, thereby always knowing its location. Very handy.

One day I had been using it on various jobs around the house and then returned it back to its resting place beside my bed. But I had misplaced the sheath. It wasn't even on my belt. I looked on the floor, behind the bedside table, under the bed—nothing. I had some clothes lying on my bed: one pair of pants, a shirt and some socks. So I picked them up, hung up the shirt and pants then put the socks in a drawer. Then I proceeded to strip the bed layer by layer to look there—nothing. The next hour or so was spent at all the locations around the house that I had visited that day, now wishing that I'd put my belt on then the sheath would've been right with me.

And yes, I located my belt too but no result. So eventually that evening I'd given up and thought I'll try an SD before bed as a last resort to show me where it was. That night I had one of the most vivid dreams ever experienced.

I was actually walking in my house along the corridor to my bedroom. I gazed around the bedroom and then walked over to the cupboard. Then opening the doors, I started shuffling through the various shirts and pants hanging there. Noticing the shirt that I previously had removed from my bed I reached out to grab it. That action invoked a sudden awakening.

Sitting upright in bed I glanced at the time: 2 a.m. That's the usual time I get woken up by spirit. So next thing here's me jumping out of bed and opening the cupboard door, looking for that shirt. I lifted it off by the hanger and examined both sides. Nothing untoward. That is until I opened it up and saw something hanging inside.

It was my Gerber sheath. The Velcro on it had attached itself inside my shirt. I must've dropped the sheath on my bed and then threw the shirt on top of it. This simply was quite amazing. Not only was I shown where it was but also had been led there participating in my own dream.

INTUITION

As I've mentioned before your level of intuition will go through the roof. This was especially evident when I did flower deliveries. I delivered mostly to private houses so this was an opportunity for a brief interaction. Some flowers were sent as a 'get well soon' and most of the time it was obvious that the person receiving them was ill. As soon as I saw the customer I could feel their pain; whether a sore neck or back or even a respiratory dysfunction, I could feel it. I knew this as I would always ask them if they were okay. They mostly would then explain their ailment which coincided with what I was feeling.

This also works in reverse. One time I was attending dinner with a few friends at a local restaurant. A woman two tables away half stood up, then fainted, collapsing onto the floor at one of the restaurant tables. Instantly I knew she was okay. People around us started to panic and I said to my friends, "It's okay, just wait." The restaurant owners rushed out and one of her friends dialled 000 asking for an ambulance. Another friend was supporting her head, making sure she was breathing.

Then almost as unexpectedly she woke up, sat upright on the floor, looked around, and then stood up as though nothing had happened. She then sat at her table and I could see her friends trying to explain what she just did. She was quite oblivious to the whole incident. I knew she was okay right from the onset of this situation.

THE LIFT

We had a new multistorey hotel open its doors to the public at one time and being so close to the beach I thought it would be a chance to see the water from a different perspective. So one weekend I took my daughter along and we waited for the lift up to the top floor to see the view along with many other onlookers. When the doors opened it was full of people who already took in the view. But half of them didn't alight so only some of us would fit to go back up.

My daughter jumped aboard with me following but abruptly I felt very uncomfortable. So I stepped out, blocking the doorway, motioning my daughter to get out too, but she would have none of it. Not wanting to cause a scene and with all the other people waiting I let the doors shut so they could be on their way. Now this was a real dilemma. Was I feeling this right? If so, am I now to be responsible for some disaster that I could've saved my daughter and perhaps many more people from? This situation felt very uneasy but how could I explain my feelings to anyone without looking like some sort of weirdo?

Anyway, the doors closed. And I looked up to view the floor level indicator. Nothing happened. One minute passed by and still nothing happened. Others around me were looking too by now and I could see them starting to talk to each other. So I walked over to the reception desk and asked them if the lift had been playing up. "No, not at all," was the reply. Then she too walked over to take a look for herself. By then it was about four minutes in and still hadn't moved. The receptionist then muttered to herself that, "Someone has pushed two buttons at once again," as she walked back to her desk and made a phone call.

The next half hour was spent with me trying to find out if everyone in the lift was okay. There was a phone in the lift for emergencies but it was only connected to the lift manufacturing supplier in the city 75 kms away. The receptionist assured me that the lift technicians were on their way but it would take some time as it was a weekend. During the next 30 minutes I discovered that this had been happening almost every day since opening. I threatened to call the fire brigade but the receptionist said they arrived the day before and could do nothing.

Anyway, the whole situation was handled very badly and at the 1.5 hour mark, just as I was about to jam a crowbar in the lift doors to open them, the techs arrived. The doors were quickly opened and out poured a crowd of very hot, dishevelled people who had uniquely bonded under stress.

Ever since that day I have learned to view intuition very seriously.

WIRED

I used to work part time at a local school doing maintenance. The school was within walking distance, being only 300 metres down the road from home. So as often as possible I'd avoid using my car. One morning, crossing the road to the school entrance, I noticed a coil of wire laying near the road centre. I picked it up, noting that it was heavy duty and probably had fallen off a tradie's vehicle. I walked up to the nearest bin, opened the lid, and immediately felt that I shouldn't throw it away. There was no real reason for this but as with other experiences I knew to trust my feelings. So I popped it in my side pocket.

That morning my first job was to clean all the roof gutters. The school was huge and surrounded by trees so this was to be a mammoth job that would probably take two weeks in total.

So I grabbed the biggest ladder, largest bucket and some gloves then made my way to the furthest outlying building to start. This building hadn't received its fair share of maintenance and the gutters had rusted through in a few spots. I started at one corner, extended the ladder and made sure it was stable, then climbed up to the first section which was around five metres high. Looking right along the gutter you could see it was jam-packed with leaf debris. I placed my bucket on the roof and put on my gloves. Just as I was about to dip into the leafy sludge with my first handful I felt very uncomfortable again.

I've learned from past experiences this needs to be addressed so I rechecked everything. The ladder was stable and the gutter it was pressing against looked good. I looked at the bucket which was sitting at an odd angle and immediately could feel the wire in my side pocket get hot. Now this was weird! I removed my gloves and pulled the wire from my pocket. It wasn't hot at all. Then looking back at the bucket, I moved it aside to see why it was sitting crooked. There were two roofing screws sitting proud of the metal roof which would be a future problem if it rained as the holes uncovered by the screw head would allow water ingress.

But that seemed secondary to what I felt I should do. Something was telling me to wrap the wire around the screws and then wind it around the nearest rung on the ladder. Which I did. This took a bit of time as I felt it should be secure. Then after this I put my gloves back on and proceeded to scrape the leaf waste out and into the bucket. After a minute it was time to move on to the next section which involved moving the ladder along about two metres. Then realising my mistake of wiring the ladder to this position I put down the bucket and pulled off my gloves.

Right then the whole gutter just collapsed. No warning, nothing! Luckily I had hold of the ladder and nothing in my hands. The ladder lurched sideways and the only thing stopping my five-metre fall was the wire on the ladder rung I had just attached to the roofing screws. I was amazed at the strength it had. The screws didn't shift even though the ladder was at an odd angle and only anchored by one leg; it was solid. So I climbed down to safety.

I could've so easily dismissed what I felt, which upon reflection scared me more than the actual event I experienced.

DREAMER

Always curious with my newfound link to consciousness, I thought to myself, is it possible to explore other dimensions? As I have stated. we are multidimensional beings, but where is the actual proof of that statement? So, when I did a SD I asked if this was possible to explore these alternate realities. The answer I immediately received was "Tonight"!

That night and ever since I have been having these vivid dreams. Sometimes a bit weird, other times almost like an alternate life I could've lived. Occasionally I recognise the areas that I'm living in, but other times it's quite psychedelic.

And I do mean 'live'; having been totally involved in another reality all night I wake up confused at first as to where I am.

Every night it's different.

I have also experienced the dream within a dream whereby I go to sleep in the dream I'm having and wake up in another. I tell you, that's one hell of an experience! Not for the fainthearted. And yes, I then go back to sleep in the second-level dream and wake up back in the first level. I asked for this five years ago. So that's 1,825 alternate realities and still counting. I think I need a break!

3. TONING

Let me explain about 'toning'. Toning is a type of verbal meditation. A conscious thought is held while a name is sung. A group of men select one person to be toned. This person then stands in the centre of the group. The group should really number at least four to be successful and should really not be more than 10 for reasons I'll explain later.

The central man selects a name for the others to tone. One-syllable names are much better than two; for example, Dave is better than David. Most men aren't practised singers. This doesn't matter. The toned name is sung in a different way to singing a song. Take a deep breath and say the name, say it for as long as you expel breath; then repeat over and over. It's much easier to do this with one syllable. Otherwise at some point as you expel breath you'll have to change tack to the second part of the name.

This is best done in a quiet, darkened place away from any noise or interference. The man to be toned asks the toners to hold a conscious thought about him as they sing his name, such as being healthy, clarity of thought, attracting wealth, etc. I recommend positive thoughts such as this because this is an extremely powerful instant force from consciousness.

As I'll explain later the Aboriginal people from outback Australia use a similar method called singing. Which is usually used for harm. Toning can be used in the same way but there are consequences, of course.

The group usually close their eyes which aids concentration and avoids distraction. You'll find at first each toner is fairly quiet saying the name but with each breath the decibels rise and with practice will become quite loud. The whole tone should last about five minutes. You will hit a loud peak for about a minute then each person will naturally become quieter.

At the end all the group must remain settled and silent, then move toward the central person and place hands on him, or a man hug, or whatever you feel. This seals the direct link and resettles the mind again.

The men involved must know each other very well and have an open line of communication. There must be trust and respect with each man involved. An openness of mind and some former experience in meditation is helpful too. Once one man is toned then the others will desire to experience this as well.

What can you expect?

Sometimes the central toned man will start off being quite unsettled in his head and there will be a lot of confusion. Not always the case, of course. But as the tone gets louder the conscious gate opens wide and the full force of the intention will start pouring through. Each man has a different experience, of course. For me, my mind space gets a complete white-out at this point. It's like being in a full-on forceful warm shower pouring directly on my head. It literally floods your soul and can be very emotional.

For the toners they will first struggle with their own sound, tying to match the other voices and holding the intention asked. But after a minute they'll hit their stride and will revel in the reverberations from each voice. After some experience the group will sound like a group of monks chanting in their church. You will feel a presence of mind which is relaxing yet quite vibrant. It's not unusual to get emotional as well. At some point all the group will be as one. All consciousnesses will be locked in and onto the intention. This is why this practice can be so enlightening and yet so harmful if used for destructive purposes.

Make no mistake, this is very powerful and as always can be used for positive or negative intentions. The positive is this way and the negative of course is used in the 'Aboriginal singing' method.

You wouldn't want to be in the centre of a tone if the toners had a negative intention towards you. That would be extremely destructive. The same with the Aboriginal method. The tribal elders will get together and sing the person's name coupled with a negative intention. I lived in a community of approximately 500 Aboriginal people where this was practised. A woman who had been overstepping her perceived importance had fallen out of favour with the elders. After being sung she was dead within two weeks. In fact, she found out she had been 'sung', which in this Aboriginal community as well as many others is basically like being told by your doctor that you have terminal cancer.

Even if you doubt your doctor, the precedent has already been set. I presume you would've experienced this with other people that as soon as the doctor diagnoses an illness that thought stays with you. If it's a terminal diagnosis, then you may as well be given a death sentence. Yes, some people are strong-willed enough to fight this and there are plenty of examples out there of people who have beaten cancers and other terminal conditions. But the majority don't.

So I hope you can see how powerful the conscious mind is. Now if you can imagine four or more conscious minds working together then that's just more power. As I mentioned before, no more than 10 people should be involved. It's hard for 10 or more to stay on subject. They can wander off consciously and end up revelling in the experience rather than pushing the intention.

This is okay if you want the experience but the central person misses out somewhat.

The Aboriginal method uses elders who number less than 10 and are all well known to each other. They have respect for each other and share a common goal. They are of middle age or older and have extreme confidence in what they do.

They will sit on the dirt in a circle. In the centre one will draw an image of the person they wish to concentrate on or will have an item of their clothing, lock of hair or something personal. They then sing the name of the person. They hold the intention of death in their minds. They picture that person lying down, breathless and lifeless. They hold this train of thought and sing in unison for up to one hour or more.

The result every time is death, usually within two weeks. Now, being a small community as most are, you could argue the fact that the intended person would somehow get wind of the fact that they had just been 'sung'. Whatever happens next the result is always the same.

So I reiterate, be very careful when you are doing toning. For your sake and for others'!

4. AUTOMATIC WRITING

Automatic writing is done to release your mind of its ego. Your ego is your persona that you have created to exist socially. There are enough books and research out there to explain what your ego is. So I will not go into depth about your ego and its function. If, however, you don't realise or recognise your own ego then this chapter will be a real awakening for you.

Automatic writing is a fairly effective method of digging away your ego and allowing the presence of what and who you are actually to surface. It's like getting to a base understanding of consciousness to a level that can be understood. As the human mind is relatively complicated, it's very hard to have a self-examination of your own mind because you will find you'll question everything you think rather than the thought telling you what it is.

Automatic writing allows you to actually expel all your ego and get down to the subject matter. It's a bit involved though so don't think there is an easy way or shortcut by using this method.

Firstly, you'll need a quiet room all to yourself. Well-lit but with no distractions, such as noise or sudden movements. A good supply of A4 or foolscap paper to write on—20 pages at least.

You'll probably be locked away for two hours or more, so no phones. Put a 'Do Not Disturb' sign on your door and lock it. Now no-one can open the door or otherwise interfere with your thoughts.

Start with a heading on your first page. Something that seems as far away as possible from your own beliefs, for example, I am love, everyone loves me, I am worthy of love, etc.

Write this down. Also make note of the time and write this somewhere. You will not look at the time again till finished. This is over when it's over, and you'll know that when it happens.

Now you have to write an answer. Then look and write the heading again and repeat this process. You can say it too. That works much better if you do. You write whatever comes into your head. No mucking around or procrastinating. If you have a blank, then write 'Blank', say it and write it! Then read and say the heading again.

So then it's on. After about an hour of talking to yourself and writing the replies you'll notice your writing hand becomes quite sore. Don't stop, keep going, you're only halfway.

Keep at it. Towards the end your mind's ego or left side of the brain will drop its cover and the right side will take over. It'll be like another person is writing the answers and you'll just be observing what they say. This is the 'automatic part'. It'll say its piece then it's over. You'll be worn out by this stage, believe me. The last statement written is your conscious self. The self with no ego representation. It can be a truly enlightening experience to discover what is at the core of your being.

When you do this you'll find your first experience will be the best so choose wisely. Subsequent writings at later intervals usually aren't as good as the first. But that is not a hardened rule, more of an observation.

Let me show the example of my first experience.

My first writing subject was the statement: Life is perfect being me.

Basically nothing at that time could be more further from the truth so in that context it was a good choice.

So, I wrote 'Life is perfect being me'. And then I wrote down the first answer that crossed my mind. 'Yes it's great I could go on'. Then I wrote the same statement again. 'Life is perfect being me'. Then answered. 'Yes fantastic really'. I started out being quite sarcastic with myself because the subject matter seemed so unrealistic. So I kept writing that statement and writing an answer.

Life is perfect being me. Yeah great.

Life is perfect being me. Yes, just one thing after another.

Life is perfect being me. Yes, brilliant.

Life is perfect being me. Yes, gigantic, great, stupendous.

Life is perfect being me. Yeah really.

Life is perfect being me. Great gargantuan.

Life is perfect being me. Brilliant bright sunny.

Life is perfect being me. Amazing great ripper.

Life is perfect being me. Great Big Blobs of it.

Life is perfect being me. Excellent, Spastic, Explosive.

Life is perfect being me. Brill, Great, Boisterous.

Life is perfect being me. Big Jobs Ahead.

Life is perfect being me. Gargantuan Jobs Ahead.

Life is perfect being me. Tops, Expecting greatness.

Life is perfect being me. Extraordinary bright envy.

Life is perfect being me. Extra big extravert.

Life is perfect being me. Unusually good.

Life is perfect being me. Upset Explosive.

Life is perfect being me. Enterprising extreme.

Life is perfect being me. Everything wants.

Life is perfect being me. Extraordinary shielding.

Life is perfect being me. Attributed to anything.

Life is perfect being me. Envious outsiders.

Life is perfect being me. Allowed to hurt.

Life is perfect being me. Incredible interruptions.

Life is perfect being me. Nasty blokes.

Life is perfect being me. Imperfect souls.

Life is perfect being me. Uninterrupted people.
Life is perfect being me. Allowed to help.
Life is perfect being me. Incredible likeness.
Life is perfect being me. Annoyed in people.
Life is perfect being me. Unless I help.
Life is perfect being me. Helping to help.
Life is perfect being me. Try to help.
Life is perfect being me. Unusual response.
Life is perfect being me. Happy response.

End of page 1 of 10.

See the sarcasm, then halfway there's a change looking inward.

So in the interests of content I shall just write the answers from now on.

PAGE 2

Helping to happy. I'm not blind. Unusually not blind. Help to me. Help me. I'll help me. Help to hold me. Bend my soul. Unless I'm bad. Help me. Unless I'm told. To help me. Help me. Unusually blind. Told me so. To help me. Help. Lost me. Scare me. Sent it to me. Send me it.

Send me. Help it so. Unusually so helps. Scare me. Sense of me. Understand me. Stand on me. Said it was so. Understand it so. Yell at me.

Hell on me. Bless me. Bury me. What's the use? Totally me. Send it to me.

End of page 2.

You can see the replies are changing to help and understanding.

PAGE 3

Bend me. Not so. Sadly so. Send it to me. Repeat once more. What's perfect? What's life? What is? What is me? Until I go. Achingly so. To be me. Until what. What. Me. I'll write an essay. I'll have me. What'll I be then. Understood then. Under me. Under a tree. Under ground. Until it's done. It's done. Until end. Until end. Ending. Pass time till I die. Unloved. Until love. Love not one. Unless I said it. Understand it. What is it. Pissed off.

End of page 3.

Now death and ending comes into play.

PAGE 4

Unhandled. Ashamed. Afraid. Until what. Unless it happens. Death isn't. I don't believe that. Don't try to understand it. Rest assured. Assholes. Not approved. What's it like. Energise it. Want to try it. Don't try to talk about it. Alone need help. Expend all opposition. I'll try harder next time. Try to help me I won't. To try is all else. To hell with all. Send it all back.

Try to tell all. Till 40. 27 over. Don't go over it. I'll tall all once. Try to kill me. To do it more. Upset all once. To death us do part. Defend me once. Allow to stand off. To die for me. Send it to me. Do not give it to me. Allow any beasts to die. Send in the clowns.

End of page 4.

Another layer gone. Exposing death.

PAGE 5

Say this is so. What's the point. Bugger it. Sausage sizzle. To be with me, not. Do not be with me. Don't understand it to me. Die with me. To tell none if you want. Hell is here too. Catch up here soon. No more being me. I'm not here. Send me alone. To hell with me. To hell come with me. Send me to hell with you. Do not go with me. Do not tell me. Don't tell me that. Send don't tell me.

Help me to do it. So you can be too. Help me to kill you. Die with me. Help me die with you. Die with me soon. Death to you with me. I'll die with you. I'll kill with you. Death waits for me. Kill or death. Bloody kill me. Until I die with you. Death with me. Death is me. I'll kill you.

End of page 5.

You can see the connection with death. It overwhelms the reactions.

PAGE 6

To die lots for. Unless I die for. Death awaits you. Kill or die with me. I'll go last. Don't believe you will. Don't give up yet. I don't know anything. Die death dead. To be death all. Die death dead. To be ended. Send death here. Protect the living. Don't let them go. Help me go. I'm gone already. I am something else.

Not who you think. To be with me now. Death 4 show. Don't go there. Dream will go not. Do not let him down again. Do help him die in vain. Not help anymore left. Don't go lots help none. Lost help alone go back. Alone help.

Alone. Stand alone no help. Alone help me alone. Help alone help alone help. Help not coming. Help me not allowed. Don't help me to help. Self-help not allowed. Help me on top of this.

End of page 6.

You can see the start of the pure conscious spirit behind the ego starting to state its case. The statement 'Help me go' is direct reference to helping my body/spirit pass over. 'I'm gone already' is the actual spirit making a statement to where it resides. 'Help me not allowed' means that the spirit cannot do certain things which the physical body would want it to.

PAGE 7

Blind help me staggering. Help no look help die dream. Lost help me lost help. Alone lost help no good help. Locked up help look help. Lost hell look help. Misery hell hole of help. To hell not me also. Can't go I'll risk dream. No risk no life dream follows. Life death risk hell help. To death knows no help.

To know what is helps me. To help who doesn't come back. So I can help one or another. So eventually I can go with them. To hell with help from me. So I can help you to refrain. So I can do it to you too. To end it all with one blow. So I can drink it all.

Lost can u think of it. So I can think of now. Send have out fa all 2. Send it here with one 2 for all. To end it with me so come. No risk to come with me. Help me to end it with you. Send help soon be it you. To hell with help I'm with you. Send no one but me for you.

To help me with you for sin. To help me be with you last. Help 2 be now and forever. Send help not now though. To kill is not to leap yet. Don't tell me to go.

End of page 7.

This shows the physical side asking the non-physical side for help passing over. But there is still confusion because of the lack of flow with coherent words.

PAGE 8

Send it help but not now please. To help is not help from me. To be all it was to be. Send help to all but me. To help but to not help me. No help for me. It's all on me. I have all hell on my shoulder. I will face it but no help offered. To end will hurt die for all. End with me now but. My god don't end it with me.

I can't go there to die yet. Today is another way out of here. Tonight I will rest and go away soon. So I will not go with you now. To are die for all best we. Don't know or respect one another. Help me don't go with me.

Don't do this or else I'm gone. Don't do this now or else. Don't do it now please. Don't go there now please. To do this or else what. Not now don't know what to do. Death help wish home with me no one else. Left earth more answer now.

Send help not gibberish lost neck. To help me you must not die or kill. Protect don't kill not die or kill. Don't go protect don't go non help. Responsible to families help them not me. Not anywhere near that. Not me. Not. Help me. Not me help me. Not anywhere near it hell.

End of page 8.

You can see the ego almost arguing with the underlying consciousness.

PAGE 9

Don't believe it core belief. Responsible go not help. I need help but won't get it. Not now it won't happen. Not really sad awaits. To do or die its over but. Unless it's over soon hell. End me now it's so slow. To get me out of here. Don't let me get out. Send help get out soon. Go soon help others first.

So I can go to as well. I am gone soon no help. I watch you hell to me. Morbid death with me awaits. I died now you too. I go I have gone your turn now. I watch you go I've gone too. I see all you before me. Tell me what I see. I show you see what I've seen. Come back with me don't go yet. I am here to watch you can't help.

Watch paid your turn can u take it. Core belief of death watcher. Death shall not touch me yet. Paid you experience I have felt all. No pain is greater than my pain. Don't tell me you can do it. I watch you tell all can't do it. I am here 4 you to watch you. My pain is harder than yours.

At this point my hand kept on writing. I watched the words develop just like it was someone else doing it. I didn't write 'Life is perfect being me' again until the next page.

This is what followed.

I will go and experience it with you until you come back. I have felt it too don't give in yet. I didn't give in. Don't go yet. You need no help. Because I don't get help & I'm alone too.

End of page 9

PAGE 10

This account of page 10 is exactly as it was written.

Life is perfect being me.

Don't go everyone goes it isn't up to me.

But I'll watch you I'll take the blame. It's my pain not yours. I'll experience your pain & mine till it's far greater. Believe me so your journey is safer. No pain is impossible. But I will lessen your pain so you can go easier. I will be beside your family. I will try to help but I am bound by things out of my control. Please understand me as I pass on all your good deeds & will to all others.

I will hold your goodness and please all others with this. I am here to help. Believe it as I believe in you. I am here to nurture your spirit.

I will not let your time on earth be in vain.

It's my duty to hold all your pain & help others withhold theirs.

You need not fear and I will be beside you. Know this and all will be at peace.

So one hour and 40 minutes later I had my statement. Direct from spirit. I encourage you to find yours.

THAT'S ALL FOLKS

So, that's the four steps completed. Doing all this takes time and dedication of course. But the benefits will far outweigh your commitment. Even the fact of reading this book so far has engaged your SP into action. The gateway has a light shining the way. You're holding the torch. I encourage you to take the first step. It could be the most important one in your life so far.

A SMALL WORD ON DEATH

Death has a benefit. May I qualify that to say if you have experienced death then you will know of the benefits I have outlined here.

Death is looked at with such abhorrence instead of it being merely a transition. Most people who die and are brought back to life have wondrous tales of beautiful places. Some are so moved they'll write a book of their experiences.

So what has happened then? They have had a complete transition into consciousness. Devoid of physical limitations. They exist in their interpretation of creation itself. Ego washes out when they transit so the clarity and creative wisdom that they perhaps never experienced is suddenly thrust into them. They are now part of the spirit that has loved them forever. Time has no significance there either.

All society's consequences are null and void. No more shrouds covering the inner you. You're totally exposed in the raw essence of the one constant. And that constant is consciousness.

Although the non-physical is a pleasant experience it can also be misinterpreted. If for example you have a death experience when you're very young, then it can have an adverse effect. For example, I was two years old when I had mine. Because I was not fully aware of the physical world in which I was born I then had an experience of the non-physical world that I wasn't expecting. So at an early age being nowhere near mentally aware of myself I had experienced both dimensions. Also the experience was quite powerful and I could manifest things in my mind and could see them with my own eyes.

Being a young child scared of things that go bump in the night didn't help either. For years I witnessed all manner of creatures lurking about my bedroom. It was so bad that I couldn't go to sleep unless my head was totally covered by blankets. So if I opened my eyes I wouldn't see the latest apparition that had come to visit.

When I was very young I'd race into Mum and Dad's bedroom but of course that didn't last long. I remember telling Mum about what I was seeing and she explained that I must be running a temperature, thus hallucinating.

If that was the case, then those temperature-induced hallucinations lasted about six years.

One of the worst nights involved small stick figures wandering through a pot plant sitting on a nearby window ledge. With the moonlight shining through I could clearly see them. Occasionally they'd stay still, masquerading as the stalks. Then after a minute they'd start moving again. I thought, I'm getting out of here, but the doorway was blocked by a large stool-mounted chrome robot with bright red eyes, its body slowly revolving on the stool. The moonlight bounced off it too, reflecting around the room.

So as you can see this experience is of little benefit when you're young. But with age and life experience the transition into and back from consciousness can be beneficial. And the ultimate complete transition is a move into raw beauty, the essence of consciousness itself.

THE DOWNSIDE

As with all things in life there is a downside with your spiritual connection. Careful attention is needed in your association with yourself and others around you. If something causes you to be angry and that anger is directed at a person then your spirit who is behind you 100% sees that person as a problem. It will act on your thoughts and immediately attack the person you are thinking about.

How does it do this? Exactly the way that toning or singing does. It concentrates on that person's spirit which then directly connects to the physical body. As I've said before it doesn't magically destroy that person but hastens the illness, disease or body dysfunction that is due to them. So the time frame that this would ordinarily happen—say about 10-20 years— gets cut down to just a few months or even weeks.

You have to be very careful; even a friend giving a cutting remark will cause your spirit to react. When this happens just sit with your emotional reaction for a brief moment, you'll immediately feel the heat inside that it generates. Now your breathing practice comes into effect. Breathe in deeply; as you breathe out imagine expelling out all this heat. Repeat till all the heat has gone. This will also help you realise that the cutting remark has no real substance, and its only existence is really your reaction to it.

Believe me when I say I speak from experience. These attacks have materialised on individuals, friends and foe over the last few years. I didn't do it on purpose. I just had no real understanding of what was happening until years later.

Also, be careful with yourself.

If you have low self-esteem or are harbouring depression, then your spirit will recognise this as a call to action. It will help you go down. It will literally dig the hole and toss you in it. A bout of depression can end up being an all-out war as your extreme negative thoughts get emphasised by your spirit helping you along the way. It jumps right in there with you and hastens your demise. As I've mentioned before I've lived through this stage in my life and it was only by luck that I pulled myself out.

And how did I do that? Just asked my spirit for help. The help wasn't immediate though; it took a few weeks. I put that down to the fact that in the bottom of that hole I was trying to figure out the easiest way to kill myself. So my spirit was helping me to do that. Then it was asked not to. It was as conflicted as I was.

There is also another downside. To knowingly or unknowingly inflict a negative outcome via spirit through consciousness is not just a one-way street. Every action has a reaction. Basic laws of physics still apply in both the worlds. So part of that negative energy that your spirit has picked up on actually is held and sent back to you.

That is why the singing method of attack is done with a group. The more people invited means the negative feedback is lessened. Each person gets a small amount compared to a single person getting the full force. It is much easier for them to handle.

As with the old argument with good versus evil, consciousness through spirit works so much better through good intention or love. It multiplies, spreads out vastly with more speed. The negative angle is actually self-generated; it goes against the grain, so to speak. It's slow and dark and pushes its way through reluctantly. This is explained much better in my book **SCI**.

OUT OF THE BLUE

One of the upside benefits of opening your connection is that it greatly enhances your current communication. Have you ever experienced a friend telling you that they were thinking of an old mate they hadn't heard of in 30 years and the next thing they got a phone call from him? Or that they were having a coffee and he was at the next table? What about his name popping up as a Facebook 'Friend of a friend'? These experiences will be commonplace with your newfound link.

So why is this happening? Consciousness is the common link. Your thoughts go straight to that person. Their spirit then finds a way to reconnect. Your spirit and theirs are now aware of each other so will bring about the circumstances for communication. Friends, old lovers, virtually anyone you start to focus on will appear seemingly out of the blue. That's what they will say to you, but you will now know why.

BIG LOVE

There is a very important side benefit to existing in the conscious field. And that benefit is love. Not love in the common sense but more about attraction from the dimension that love exists in. If you practise the Secret, then men and women will be attracted to you within this dimensional field. Now I'm not saying sexual attraction, as that will need your input. But the dimension that love exists in knows no human boundaries. So it just spreads out and people of like-minded influence are attracted like a moth to the flame.

If you are searching for a partner or not, they will appear to you as you go about your normal day-to-day activities. Shopping, working, going to a café or gym. Whatever. So if you are looking for that certain someone, don't worry, they'll appear in your life. No need for dating sites, pubs or other public fishing grounds.

Only problem is once they appear then it'll be pretty hard trying to ignore them and like me you'll end up getting married ... but that's up to you.

Either way you will experience much stronger connections with not only humans but all other animals, plants, rocks and everything that exists in your dimension. You have walked into the stream of consciousness. Revel in its flow, you'll never want to leave.

THAT LIGHT

When you practise the Secret consistently you will notice something quite strange when you close your eyes. In your mind's eye, right in the centre of your forehead, there will be a tiny light. This is particularly noticeable at night when you're in bed trying to get to sleep. You will also notice it when you are being toned. It will be brighter though and the man hug at the end will almost cause a white-out. Don't be alarmed! You're not going nuts!

Have you ever heard the phrases 'Light at the end of the tunnel' or 'I've seen the light'? What about people who say they've had a death or near-death experience, claiming they experienced a bright white light?

This IS that light.

You are experiencing the actual light from the non-physical dimension. It's a bridge between the two, actually. This is the link and you've opened the door, so to speak.

Here is your proof that this part of you exists. Once you see it you can appreciate the absolute beauty in the fact that you are just so much more than your physical existence.

You are now seeing what most people only get to see when they die. I hope you realise how beneficial this link is to you and everyone else you interact with.

It is especially useful when your own time has come to leave this physical plane as you can determine your own euthanasia. Your time will be in your hands, not determined by someone else, and all you'll have to do is ask.

SCHIZOPHRENIA

After a few months practising the Secret you'll notice that the actual ritual is no longer needed. The four stages that you had practised will have morphed into an automatic connection. Your own willpower then determines the direction.

At this stage it's highly likely that your SP will ask to join you in real time; that is, to enter your mind and experience your physicality. It doesn't actually ask. You will be compelled to do this. The various implications and subsequent possibilities this entails would need a complete book to explain. Once in it doesn't leave. This event will certainly increase your understanding of schizophrenia. You'll have two identities existing in the same mind space. For the first time you'll be aware of what it can actually do. Mere mortals won't understand. The power you'll possess is on one hand a perfect tool and on the other a loose cannon.

Be aware of how you feel at all times. As I've said before, if you're angry be aware of what the consequences are. Love and compassion that was once a trickle will turn into a raging torrent if you desire. You'll have much more control of your life situation and at the same time you'll really start enjoying the ride. Everything will start to change.

So buckle up, brace yourself, hold on tight and enjoy the ride.

David Zachary Smith

COMMON GROUND

To bathe in truth with other men
Devoid of ego, stripped of judgement
I honour the integrity sacrificed
Immersed in the Common Ground

COMMON GROUND

In 2008 I, along with nine other men, attended our first meeting of Common Ground, a special workshop put together by Men's Health and Wellbeing, Queensland, Australia. Founded 20 years ago it has recently been renamed Men's Wellbeing. We met in a small community hall from 7–9.30 p.m. each Tuesday night for eight weeks.

We had three facilitators who guided us along the various courses they had arranged. The whole workshop was basically designed to have men open up, to talk about their lives. To share their feelings in a totally open environment.

Ours was one of the first held in Queensland and was such a success that there have been many more since. This started a whole new facet in my life and has been a direct life-altering catalyst ever since.

Firstly, a basic set of rules were agreed upon to allow each of us to be received openly. They were:

Confidentiality – what is said in the circle remains in the circle.

Respect – for yourself and each other.

Honouring – acknowledging all aspects of ourselves and knowing that all aspects are welcome.

Responsibility – for yourself and your actions.

Listening – being present for each man.

No Interrupting – advice is not given unless it is requested.

Punctuality – respecting the times agreed upon: 6.45 for a 7 p.m. start.

Acceptance – of each man for who he is and where he is.

All Feelings Okay – everything is welcome.

Integrity and Honesty – with yourself and with other men.

No Substances – men having partaken in non-prescription drugs or alcohol will not be welcome that week.

Commitment – to yourself and to the group to be here each week.

Sense of Fun – a willingness to share your humour.

All of us were unknown to each other and it was for me very confronting to be put under the spotlight, so to speak. But that was more a feeling of insecurity. Each meeting began with what they called **check-in**, whereby each man would discuss what happened to them in the previous week. The facilitators guided us by firstly telling their own stories which were quite frank and open. That encouraged each of us to be more exposed in relating our own situation. After doing the night's course we then had a **checkout** which allowed each of us to say what we thought of the course and anything else that popped up.

We explored topics such as:

Real men: What it is to be a so-called real man in society today.

Mentors: What effect they have in building character.

Emotions: What role they have in expressive thought.

Relationships: How do we increase our awareness of what's going on?

Masculinity: Is it really important?

Risk: How adverse we are to risk and its consequences.

'Fixing it' with your father: You cannot get on with your life successfully until you have understood him, forgiven him, and come in some way to respect him.

Finding sacredness in your sexuality: Sex will either be a sleazy and obsessive part of your life or a sacred and powerful source of wellbeing.

Meeting your wife on equal terms: In a modern marriage soft men get left and bullies drive self-respecting women away.

Engaging actively with your kids: You can't be a parent from behind a newspaper and you can't leave it all to your wife because a woman doesn't have all the ingredients needed.

Learning to have real male friends: You will have to get emotional support from other men and find out how to complete your own initiation into manhood.

Finding your heart in your work: You will need to find work you can believe in, so that the time and energy of your working life is spent in a direction where your heart lies.

Freeing your wild spirit: You will need to find a spiritual basis for your inner life that is specifically masculine and based in nature, which connects you to the earth you live on.

At one stage we had to present our parents to the group. One week for fathers, the next for mothers. Each man would take centre stage with a photo and talk about what their parent did and more importantly meant to them. That certainly opened up a can of worms for half of us, including myself. Very confronting when you can finally tell the truth about your childhood or otherwise.

And every week we were left with some homework to ponder over. It was such an enlightening course that most of us wanted to keep the meetings up.

So almost every fortnight since we have had a meeting right up to the present day. I wrote an account of each meeting which was emailed to each member so no one would miss out on what was done. This was originally intended to keep everyone informed and as a base to what we had covered. Now I offer all these to the reader in the hope that some enlightenment will be gleaned from these following pages.

People have dropped out, of course, including myself for two years, but I have returned to write these memoirs. A testament to these men who gave themselves the chance to be open.

Dates and times are displayed and every time I attended I wrote a recollection of what was discussed. These are presented here as a guide that will help other men take action with their own lives.

Each fortnight we would turn up at someone's house (place), and after a brief greeting we'd start with a check-in then follow with a subject agreed upon two weeks beforehand, then finish with a checkout. As meetings started at 7 p.m. and ran to 9.30– 10.00, or longer sometimes, we would always have a tea break.

It should be mentioned that a 'token' ornament (talking stick) was used and held by each person in turn. This signified that he had the floor and couldn't be interrupted. When a man said "HO" that signified that he had said his piece. He'd then place the talking stick back on the table for another man to pick up. In the last few years Morgan had a special one made, a modern artefact made in the tradition of the Cherokee Indians. A fine piece of natural wood decorated with feathers on top, fur in the middle and snake skin on the bottom. It also has painted images of a scorpion, chameleon and a shell. It is still used to this very day. When I have the meetings at my place I do prefer to use a 'killer boomerang' given to me by the Warlpiri's of Lajamanu.

Our numbers have varied over the years. Half the original members are still here. At one time we had new men join in but they too have left. So now we have whittled down to five members and we are laxer with our rules. Subjects aren't used anymore as one usually appears during check-in. If it doesn't we always have something new to discuss as we each work/live in quite diverse areas. But ultimately the respect is still there and this allows us to be totally open.

The following write-ups are the unedited copies from all our meetings so far. In respect of the men participating I have changed their names to protect their privacy.

Please enjoy these memoirs.

Common Ground
2008

The first meeting was at Cody's house on June 3, 2008. However, the first recorded meeting was as follows.

Scott's Place Oct 8, 2008

Secret Meeting

Hello, guys.

At first we were three. Scott, Cody and myself. During check-in, lights from a dark stealth machine made by a WW2 aircraft factory in Asia appeared down Scott's driveway. As its heat-affected turbine wound down out stepped the pilot ... Morgan. Morgan explained that his new friend 'Tom Tom' gave him the wrong directions and I fear that Tom's life may be short-lived.

That was not the only manifestation from the night. As we all discussed the deep and meaningful, a strange beam of light caught our attention. It seemed to appear from around the dam and danced through the trees and bushes towards us. There was a faint mechanical noise emanating from it and it moved fairly quickly.

Suddenly the light cut out and Roger appeared in its place.

These plus many other realisations and occurrences happened that night but they shall remain a secret.

See you all at the next meet, possibly at Colin's. I have texted him but no reply as yet.

Seeya, Dave of the bush

PS. Hey, Greg, you were missing again?????

Matt's Place Nov 5, 2008

Hi, guys.

I'm getting too relaxed at our fortnightly get-togethers! If I had a sleeping bag I could have slept on Matt's couch last night.

Our meeting started with 'comfort zones' then morphed into relationships. And I reckon we all emptied some @#$$%^^&**^ out of our systems.

May I wish you all some complete clarity before our next meet!

Seeya, Dave of too much comfort

Dave of Kuluin

Cody's Place Dec 3, 2008

And then there were four!

Communication was the theme. And Cody facilitated some Compassionate Communication to us all. (Don't worry, this will all become clearer after Manshine). He did a great job which will bide him well with workshops he'll be doing in the future. I realised I communicate by not communicating. And if that makes sense you know me too well.

The night filled rapidly and by checkout this topic had only just been scratched. We probably needed twice the time to really dig into a subject that really is the base for all interactions with humans. (My dog and I understand each other very well, and that only takes a look.)

See you all next year ... I can't make the next meeting but would be happy to hold the first one in '09.

Seeya, Dave of '08

Dave Dec 6, 2008 Final

Thank you so much for participating in our men's group.

I feel that as we collectively search for truth this affects every group member. This effect moves via our families/friends to the outside world. The pattern exponentially expands.

To think that you can influence someone's life by simply thinking differently has been a wakeup call for me. It reminds me how we are so connected with everything and everyone on the planet. Every time I alter my thinking, that alone completely changes my current reflection of myself. That reflection I see is all there is, for in my mind, that is the world, everything.

Before my journey this year all I knew about ego was that, as in the Skyhooks song, it wasn't a dirty word. Now I can recognise when it kicks in. When it wants to fight. Sometimes I feel I can nearly deplete its hold on me. When my ego left my relationship, there was no-one to get upset, no-one to react. There was only someone who was a part of everything. And the seriousness of my current life situation dilated. For it had no urgency, no real meaning.

I have also picked up a golden rule: "Don't take yourself so seriously!"

Enough of myself.

Onto my Christmas wish for all you guys!

My greatest wish for you all is stillness.

I experienced this for myself twice this year, both times less than a minute. After these brief episodes the next few days ran so well that it was like I scripted it.

To grab that darkness in your mind and fall into it. To let go, visit that unconscious void that we enter during deep sleep, but to visit it consciously while awake.

To me that was the greatest gift this year and I wish it for you all.

Oh, bugger, talking about myself again!

Merry Christmas, guys.

2009

Dave's Place Jan 27, 2009

Hello, guys.

Unusual night last night. After 7 p.m. Matt turned up and we waited ... and waited ... no one ... so just the two of us ... 30 minutes later our lonely egos kicked in which reluctantly led us on a pub crawl.

Don't get offended by this as Australia Day has only just passed and many major decisions have been made by world leaders while partly intoxicated in pubs. So we had our meeting in this nightclub which unusually had many blokes present. Now I haven't been out in years but I'm surprised that women don't frequent these places anymore.

Anyway, halfway through our meeting Matt excused himself to relieve the effect of around five litres of beer. Well, that's what I thought happened, but being 'three parts' myself my memory is a little dulled in this area.

I never saw Matt again and I hope he got home all right. Luckily a bloke offered me a lift in the wee hours. He was a bit strange, claiming he was some sort of magician. He claimed he could turn me into anything. So halfway home he touched my leg and I turned into a motel!

(Cheap joke, I know, but it's early in the year.)

Anyway, I reckon as far as a meeting goes it went well and as soon as I find out where we went I'll arrange us to get there next fortnight. God bless, Davo.

Matt's Meeting Feb 5, 2009

The night's title could have read 'Manifestations' 'Follow your passion' or 'Express your feelings'. Matt set the scene and lit a candle in the three-figure idol positioned in the centre of our table, the reflections of which danced above us on the ceiling, representing our spirits watching over us.

Roger brought a book along and read a paragraph or two about expressing your feelings. Not doing this results in inner turmoil or, as stated by Cody, "Disease". Holding onto foul thoughts or negativity holds our physical being in that state. The only result of that state of 'being' can be ill-health.

Interesting that Matt's book he is currently reading was in the same vein. That is, by not following or suppressing a 'passion' over the years will manifest chronic ill health, in that case cancer.

We all had a story about the subject and it was a most interesting night.

When I finally went to bed at 11.30 p.m., after making lunch for the next day and ironing clothes, that little voice said to me, "Open your book." I have three beside my bed and I was drawn to the one named *Callings*. And I thought, I'm buggered, you've got to be kidding! I'm not going to read at this hour. I've got to be up at 5.30 a.m.! But the voice insisted. So I opened up the book and proceeded to read the next chapter.

It was called 'Obey your Thirst'. It was all about bringing passion into your life. It stated 'Repression of the Life Force is the most common reason that people seek therapy'.

By ignoring our passions, we cut ourselves off from a vigorous source of calls. Passions become needs, and if they are not met they soon become symptoms of one sort or another.

Sometimes we feel our passion is unobtainable. So we cut it off, don't go there.

Meanwhile a dam full of depression is rising up inside. But just give in a little. You may not get it all but can allow just a little bit.

It goes on to say be careful that your passion is not turned into a career or a commodity or something you take to the bank. This can kill it off.

Sometimes I'm amazed that we are so connected to each other but don't even realise it. Mind you though, I'm well on the way to thinking that something else realises this common thread and wants us to stay together.

Thanks for a great evening, Matt, I would have liked to sleep on that deck ... what a beautiful night!

Roger or Scott ... your turn next!

Seeya, Dave of US.

Ramblings Feb 8, 2009

The wall of change!

I'm interested in the point where you 'hit the wall'. You know where the situation gets so uncomfortable that you do something and change on a different path or direction.

For that new path to happen though a whole set of new circumstances need to line up to action this.

For example, the last meeting at my house Colin remarked how he was uncomfortable in the pool. I was too. If you remember he said that at a certain point a small foam joiner (noodle joiner) hit him in the head and he placed it under his neck. Then all was fine ... it was as if he asked for it and it was delivered. Well, I was the deliverer. I was uncomfortable in the pool too. But my underlying feeling was to make sure that you guys were getting the full benefit of the experience.

Right at the time I peaked in discomfort, I was floating right next to Colin. I didn't know this as I had my eyes closed. I just know right at that time was the point of no return and I ditched the foam joiner. I saw it float to a person's head then closed my eyes again trying to get into the 'zone'. My discomfort ended right before his did. I mean, I could have been somewhere else floating next to another person as I had been doing. But at that point next to Colin it was time to change.

I just wonder if that can be extended to a number of circumstances that lead to an event. There comes a point when the dominant thoughts line up then a channel of events unfold.

Ego vent!

I must tell you all of the events of a week ago. I talked about ego and thought patterns last week but neglected to give this example. I'm hooked into the Manshine Site and so I receive and sometimes join in the talks online. I had just received the annual Darwin Awards from a mate and as always found them interesting enough to pass on. If you don't know about these, they are in reference to Charles Darwin. How evolution eliminates the idiots from the gene pool. For some unconscious reason I sent the Darwin Awards onto the site.

I didn't realise this till next day when one of the most respected members wrote: "What's this bullshit, mate?"

Well, that fired everyone up. There were emails in all directions. Most of which were having a go at this response. It was like the catalyst for everyone to vent their opinions on what is firing off their ego online. It was actually very interesting to watch unfold. The emails kept firing for about five days.

What I was more interested in was that I can't see how I had sent this onto the site. The records show that I did it of course but the decision to do it was not done by me. It was almost like this anger on the site needed to vent and I was the link for that to happen ...

That interests me as I hope for you guys too ... if not, then just chalk this down to more mad ramblings from you know who ...

Colin's Place Feb 11, 2009

Well, as they say in poker, I love a full house! And that's what we had at Colin's place. I, and as was commented by the men, just felt so good there, very welcoming.

The check-ins were long but informative. We still have so much to catch up on. I suddenly realised this morning that I could have added an interesting snippet of info that happened last fortnight, which I will put on a separate post.

Title for the night could have read 'Truth and Dreams'. I would like to give you some quotes from my book *The Power of Intention*. So this is live email, I'm opening the book and yes, Buddha is first up.

I have a quote from Buddha: "Those who have failed to work toward the truth have missed the purpose of living." And as I open another page I see: "You are not this body, you are not this mind, you are the spirit ... this is the greatest truth."

As for dreams, I prefer the word 'Intentions'. Open book ... quote from Colinos Castaneda: "In the universe there is an immeasurable force which Sharmans call intent, and absolutely everything that exists in the entire cosmos is attached to intent by a connecting link."

Interesting that Greg mentioned that he feels so good with his bare feet on the sand. Apparently the Earth vibrates at 80 megahertz. (please correct me if I'm wrong there) and that is also the frequency of the mind in meditation. To feel that through your feet suggests to me that the vibration is connecting directly to you.

And Colin ... you're 'online'; good to see. When Greg gets a chance he'll post your email to us all.

Seeya, Dave of Us.

Roger's Place March 14, 2009

Mixed bag this week ... from movies and movie stars to relationships and performances. Roger did a reading about marriage from Bruce Lee's autobiography. It showed that he was pretty switched on. About marriage being a friendship struck a chord with me. That's what mine is. The problem is the spark that's missing then finds a way in from outside our relationship.

Honouring in relationships was discussed and that seems a difficult area with some of us. Scott and Roger demonstrated juggling ... singing was mentioned but not followed through. Even Kiwis collectively talked about!

Scott's on a diet for all of us. Thanks, Scott; we'll observe then learn, the cheat's way.

Roger's setting has plenty of spirit. And the roaring wind with a backdrop of frogs and crickets set the scene for a very relaxing evening. Probably too relaxing as most of us were really tired.

Last week we were so connected. But for me there was a disconnection this week. I think it's because we seem to all be readjusting to a different phase in our lives. But our ability to look in. To be the observer of ourselves has not diminished. And I think that is getting stronger.

Time will tell. Dave.

Cody's Place March 24, 2009

Trust.

A choice of gems was offered for check-in, and with each selection came a link to past lives.

Cody the psychic bloodhound picked up the trail and proclaimed that trust was a common thread this week.

Do we trust? Are we trusted? Are we facing this alone? Or is someone trusting us but not showing themselves?

How does trust lock into self-esteem? Can we not trust others till we have the ultimate trust in ourselves, the faith to face adversity, the day to day, the unknown, our family and our life?

Is trust a mere reflection? Is our lack of trust reflected through others or does our complete trust just help our lives run in harmony? These are questions asked of ourselves.

A young girl called Michelle came down to exercise our emotions ... We started with massage and led to bursts of energy, shouting, and force. Tugs of war and fists of rage followed this. Background music emphasised our feelings. Eventually hot and sweaty we calmed down, centred ourselves with rest.

Checkout followed honouring a great experience shared with our hosts.

Thank you for that experience, Cody and Michelle. Trust, faith, self-esteem.

Dave's Meeting April 7, 2009

Three stories.

Tonight's meet was held at the surf club in Mudjimba. At first I was so disappointed. The beach was a mess. High tide, froth, sticks, huge waves and strong winds. Not a good base for me to introduce the men to the 'Shout'. The 'Shout' is done by holding onto an ego-driven emotion. Best done with anger. We would be yelling and running/exercising in the sand. Finishing with a heartfelt meditation. And a call to a purpose within.

But it was not to be. We could have done it at the club, but the yelling would have brought unwanted attention. Plus, the atmosphere just wasn't quite right for that.

We were only three. Me, 'Dave', Morgan and Roger. After check-in there formed a direction on focus. What we tend to focus on was probably keeping us from seeing what IS really important. And yes, relationships turned up yet again. But we heard a different side to the norm. Each man gave his story of how he met and was attracted to his partner/wife. Three quite different stories. Very liberating to hear how each of us chose the paths we still walk along.

For me a point of clarity. I realised my permanent pattern. It has ruled and guided my various relationships my whole life. Mine is the rescuer, the lifesaver. And I can see how that removes the responsibility of the one to be rescued the ability to sort themselves out. Prevents that growth in my partners.

Thank you, Morgan and Roger, who also gleaned a little more from life's lessons on the night. The bond is strong, guys. May we all enjoy Easter. Time of rebirth, new beginnings.

Morgan's Place April 21, 2009

A night of reflection and meditation.

Men, a really meaningful and enriching night was had by all. Starting with a particularly deep check-in where the progress we have all made and insights expressed was evident to all.

Then, a guided meditation on tape from Hayley (Morgan's wife), featuring a quiet space where we could reconnect with somebody from our past. Following evening tea (including some delicious food provided by Hayley), we did an exercise writing a letter to a meaningful someone with our non-favoured hand. This proved to be worthwhile and the men took the opportunity to read their letters to the group and reflect upon their content.

After a checkout, the night ended. In summary, a night that reinforced the importance of the group to us all.

Next meeting, Scott's (TBC).

Cheers, Morgan.

Scott's Place May 5, 2009

Six men arrived to Scott's place.

At check-in it was evident that the previous meeting at Morgan's was still vivid in our men's minds. After, Scott's intention was spoken and his suggestion of a walk followed by free discussion rang true with us all.

Walking the drive. We walked along Scott's drive in silence except for our gravelly footsteps and the occasional 'click' which immediately preceded a flash of light from a torch illuminating a puddle. The wind made itself heard through the gum trees as the cumulus clouds raced over the moon's face. At mid-point we stood in silence as the wind accelerated and one of the many cloud fronts decided to sprinkle us with $H2O$. For me I had to close my eyes to realise the full effect. To be at one with nature at least briefly. We returned to a cuppa break.

Our discussion centred on 'observation' of ourselves and others. Controlling forces and spiritual guidance rated a mention. Also the realisation that all we really can satisfy is feelings and needs. I keep reporting of the importance of our group. It cannot be taken lightly. For a chance to say the truth that doesn't leave the circle makes us verbalise our thoughts, gives them meaning. Our experiences of life have a common thread but they are miles apart in reality.

Thank you, Scott, always a pleasant and calming place to meet which is an obvious reflection of you. Next meeting is at Colin's. After that Matt's place.

Colin's Meeting May 19, 2009

A full house at Colin's place. So good to see all his family there too. And may I say what fantastic boys he has.

Money and sexuality.

Interesting topics that could be talked about in great detail.

A reading from Colin kicked us off on the money path. Each man remarked how money is for him. Some say how it's spent perhaps relates to the way he was brought up.

Also that we are beings of 'flow'. That money can flow through us sometimes in a trickle or even a torrent. And perhaps if we don't keep an eye on it then none of it sticks.

Roger's reading from Bruce Lee's book told how if you do something you love and are good at it then the money will flow. From that I suppose we could swap the word money with success.

Sexuality was talked about and Roger's book stated that new or young love was like a bright flame compared to mature love being a hot bed of coals.

Each man had different experiences but a consensus was reached when we agreed that sex in a 'heart' space was probably one of the best experiences between two people.

I hadn't much to say as my inexperience in any loving area has been very lacking. But in time I hope to correct that.

Thank you all our men for sharing tonight.

Great input and a great environment to share it in.

Thanks, Colin.

Greg's Meeting June 2, 2009

Patterns from childhood.

A tight group of three men met at Greg's place.

During check-in, as mostly happens, a subject kept rearing its head. We were all dealing with the inherent learned behaviour of our past. This is then projected right into our present relationships. Eckhart Tolle would say that if you're intensely present then these patterns or learned behaviour don't exist.

But it's very hard to extinguish a learned trait. I think if you can recognise it then that's half the battle. The other half is remaining present enough not to project it on.

We then talked about how our pattern is then projected on to our kids. How we place them in our own shoes, so to speak, at that stage in our own childhood. It was good to dance around this subject and being a small group we could fully express ourselves. What also helped was the food and drink provided by Greg's family. Especially the muffins!

Thank you, Greg, another good night. Very satisfying.

Matt's Meeting June 16, 2009

Hi, guys.

This broadcast courtesy of McDonald's, Mooloolaba. Open 24 hours. Guess where I'll be for my free internet from now on???

Communication!

What a valuable tool we are presented with. So many different ways to communicate with each other. Talk, touch, face expression, seating position; hell, some of us were nearly asleep.

And the subjects: family, kids, fathers, mothers, wives, partners, work foes, bosses, ourselves. Are we really communicating effectively? Or does ego cloud over what IS really there? Is there someone there who we can tell everything to? Someone who understands? If we are spirits in this material world, then does it really matter?

Then Scott reminded us of the stars. Are we really that significant in the overall scheme of things?

Roger reminded us of the conflict happening elsewhere on Earth. The atrocities committed. Do WE really have any problems?

Who am I to judge that? Can I be philosophical over a strawberry thickshake? I think not! Just so glad of the interaction, guys. You saved me tonight! Thank you.

And safe travels men. Holidays in three of the four directions. North (Roger). South (Colin). West (Scott). And East, well the rest of us are living there so we'll keep the fort open. The bond is still there, guys.

Safe journeys ... look for signs ... written and unwritten.

Thanks, Dave of Maroochydore!

Morgan's Place June 30, 2009

Well, it's the BIG Lotto night with 90 million at stake. Who's going to be lucky? And luck played a role in our meeting too.

Only three of us tonight. Morgan, Matt and I. After check-in Morgan played a CD by

Tammy Irvine called *Meditation/Relaxation*. It worked on me. Everybody relaxed as she talked us through the process. She was so good that Matt went to sleep. Morgan and I decided to carry on the meeting at a quieter tone but luckily he eventually woke up.

Morgan then did a reading from Andrew Matthews' book *Follow your Heart*. The story reflected on 'luck' as in good or bad. It really depends on your perception. Things happen in our lives, good and bad. But some people's lives are horrific! Can we really benchmark ourselves to this idealism?

We also delved into compassion. How to show it or how does it come about in a man's life? Does it start from within? Or do you force it out there? How can you show kindness to others and be absolutely genuine?

Morgan also raised a good point about 'acknowledgement'. It might be a good idea to put one member each fortnight on a pedestal, so to speak. All the other men will say a short piece on what they admire about him. All these facts will be written on a card and presented to him on the night. Honouring is very important. Every man needs this. It needs to be done.

What do you guys think?

Thanks again, Morgan. And also to your wife Hayley who always is helping in the background.

Dave.

Dave's Place July 14, 2009

And then there were two!

Greg joined me tonight for an informal meeting at my new place of residence.

After check-in we discussed this new idea of 'honouring' the men in the group further. The important aspect being 'self-esteem'.

And that topic was given much talk and thought as we continued the evening. We both realised that there have been substantial shifts in our being since on this journey with our men's group. Also that it's good to be really challenged occasionally to help give us more momentum to shift.

Such a learning experience this life. So blessed to be alive. Let's make the most of it!

See you all at Greg's in two weeks.

Ho to that.

Thanks, Dave of M/Dore.

Roger's Place Aug 11, 2009

The Roger Report (soon to be released online), five men present.

Roger held the meeting in the backyard. We sat near this magnificent fire. I can qualify that as a 'white man's fire'. After living on two Aboriginal communities outback I know that's what they'd call it. Huge fire, plenty of heat, lots of fuel. Not cooking anything. It was just great. Framed by a bush setting on a clear starlit night. So clear that you could see the 'milk' in the milky way. I don't see that in Maroochydore.

Tonight's meeting formed a title of 'The Truth'. Or as Scott said, "What is the truth if not your perception of it?" Even at check-in two accounts related directly to the truth. And to see that truth for what it actually is can really set you free.

Scott turned up approximately halfway through and he had an interesting story relating to a work incident. To actually find the truth in that incident is really all that's important. The rest can be just a political dance.

How hard is it to say the truth? Can we be really honest with our partners or other people we interact with? If we say the real truth can we be held accountable for the outcome? I think if we have the truth then that's all that is real. Everything else is error or a grey area.

But the hardest or easiest for some people is the truth within. The actual truth of who and what you are. Are you entirely honest with yourself? If you are then you can be entirely honest with each person you interact with. Another great meeting.

Thank you, Roger, Morgan, Scott and Cody.

Dave of Maroochydore.

Matt's Shed Aug 25, 2009

Tonight's meeting was at the SIS (Sacred Industrial Space, as Greg calls it) or better known as Matt's shed.

We totalled five in all. And it was a very special night for honouring as Greg was in the limelight.

Check-in saw a similarity with three of the guys. A common thread of, let's say, scrutiny or micro-management. I have experienced this too from my partner and I must admit it just doesn't really seem necessary or warranted.

After this Greg was honoured. And may I say all the guys did a great job. I was very proud of the truth that was said. Morgan had brought along a written honouring from Scott and Roger too so no one missed out. He also supplied the framed honour sheet that was really a nice touch. Each man could then write their piece so Greg could have it on display. I think many aspects were covered of Greg and we are so glad that he is in our group. The very fact that I can write about this meeting is thanks to Greg making this site possible for us! He's a worthy man.

Can I say that this group is making it possible to look at our lives? And we all know what we have to face. For the things we don't know they'll be presented to us, usually by way of our partners. For they will reflect the lessons we need to learn in order to grow. And grow we will. How do I know? The mere fact that we are in this group tells me so.

I encourage us all to look in where we don't want to go. For that is the lesson that is most needed.

Thank you, Dave of M/Dore.

Greg's Place Sept 8, 2009

Present were Greg, Matt, Roger, Morgan, Scott and Dave via Skype.

Tonight's meeting had two purposes.

One to honour Roger and the other to talk about fear.

It was great to honour Roger, our 'wise man' of the group. I hope he really benefitted from it.

Fear is an emotion that manifests in different forms in all of us. Maybe the feeling of fear itself is quite the same but it shows itself in varying physical forms.

Do fears always stem from a childhood interaction that was never really addressed?

Or can they evolve and show up later in life with no real early connection?

Are they there to show us a lesson?

Or are they here as a natural protection mechanism to keep us safe?

So what are we to do? Face them and see that they have no hold, or perhaps the opposite? Or avoid them and be satisfied that they are just a part of our makeup? Learn to live with them and maybe they'll lose their power?

I fear that I may not have addressed this subject as wholly as possible. But I'll address that by facing that this is just a short wrap-up.

Less fear for all our men, I say.

Thank you David of Tyers Victoria (done via Skype).

Roger's Sacred Shed Oct 6, 2009

Men.

Tonight we met at Roger's 'sacred shed'. Present: Morgan, Scott, Greg, Matt and Roger. After/during check-in, we spoke at length about the future direction of the group, what it meant to us and what form it should take. We agreed we should encourage Colin and Cody to attend when they can—with Matt's sister babysitting Cody's son to help him out. We agreed to be open to another couple of men joining the group—ideally having already completed Common Ground.

In summary, those present (and Dave via Matt) agreed that the group still played an important role and it should continue. Ideally, a topic will be proposed prior to the meeting and that whenever possible the men would try to attend (Dave via Skype if he cannot be present). For each man the group has a different value—but the key is that it still does have a valuable role to play in each man's life.

Honouring will continue: next will be honouring Scott at Morgan's house on Tuesday Oct 20.

If you cannot make it—please let me know!

PS. It is Greg's birthday next meeting!

Topic: How to avoid gossiping/backbiting.

See you then.

Cheers, Morgan.

Cody's Place Oct 22, 2009

Four men at the meeting tonight (Cody, Colin, Greg and Dave) and as always Cody had a process to challenge us. And also a stark reminder where our group is heading ... where? ... then read on!

After our collective check-in it was apparent that we are all in various stages of truth in our relationships. And that truth unfortunately has resulted in varying degrees of separation. But if that is the truth within us then that's all there is. And we can be happy that we're fortunate to see it, and act on it.

Cody did a reading from a book about co-dependency. And we then wrote down what lessons, teachers and guides life is throwing at us. Then after the break we wrote down five things that we are grateful for about ourselves.

Thanks for that, Cody. I'll always remember you for going the extra mile with the group.

At checkout I gave a quote from Roger Thompson (Men's Health leader): "If someone is complaining about not getting enough from the group then they should consider putting more in than just pulling out". Well, Cody and Colin are pulling out from the group. They are not complaining. Their workload with the kids has just doubled and they both said that they can't honour the group anymore. Which is a bummer as they are due to be honoured soon, I guess. But I can't talk. My next meeting will be via Skype again. So I'm not physically present either.

I just feel that the group is about to change. I hope it lasts. But the feeling is it may not!

Can I have someone put their hand up for the next meeting?

Thank you, Dave.

Nest Reunion Nov 18, 2009

Guys ... it's been so long. I am so grateful to see you again. And what a fantastic meeting.

There was Matt (it was his nest), Scott, Roger, Morgan, Greg on paper, and myself.

Check-in was very interesting again. One of us has made a substantial shift in his life, and I honour him for his courage. Greg left a check-in for Roger to read and he channelled him very well.

Speaking of honour. It was Morgan's turn. He took the truth well. What a wonderful man we have amongst us. So valuable to our group. I was going to say we are lucky, but we attracted each other. He to the group and the group to him. So it's not luck but destiny. It was already 'written', if you like. Roger honoured Morgan on behalf of Greg.

I also had the opportunity honouring Scott. I missed out the last time so that was special for me. Such strength of character and of spirit. Another man we are so fortunate to be written to us.

The subject for tonight introduced by Scott. 'Who am I', what is the real me?

The input was just great, guys. It's clear a lot of thought was put into this. Some men could state who they are and others danced around the subject. I, as usual, tried to boil it down to its basics. Love seemed to be the underlying base reached by us all. To have love as the base for all existence is an enlightening idea, or is it an enlightening truth? My hope is that we can all feel absolute love for ourselves. And that feeling to be very strong. Because that will reflect around the group and will take us to a level which we wouldn't even dream of.

I can feel my ego kicking in so I do apologise. It wants me to repeat my statement from 'spirit':

"I am you, you are we, and we are one."

Good luck at the next meet, guys. Looks like it's at Scott's. Matt's turn to be honoured!!! Seeya, I won't be there unfortunately. Dave of Adelaide (soon).

Scott's Shed Dec 1, 2009

And so it comes to pass, guys ... another year gone! Has that gone quickly or what?

Present at Scott's shed were Scott, Roger, Morgan, Matt and myself.

Why the shed? Well, we finally received some rain. Which was falling lightly at first during check-in until Roger spoke. Then it pelted down, resonating on the tin roof. Roger fought well and we all just managed to hear him. Roger also channelled Greg again. He does this so well that I think Greg could have more time off if he likes (joking).

The topic was blockages. Matt headed us off down the path and elaborated the subject and what it means to him very well. The topic mainly centred around the mind and the blocks you mentally create for yourself. Roger did some writing on the subject and reminded us of all the physical blocks we contend with every day. Everything from information devices to paperwork, even basic household clutter. That struck a chord with Scott and he'll be throwing out his old holey socks. But only if he can find a place that sells them! Better still, with Xmas around the corner I'm sure some will arrive as presents.

Matt was honoured tonight. Words such as integrity, truth and courage filtered through our various readings. We all admire him for being so balanced and strong as he tackles his life head on. It's so important to have him with us. Stay strong, mate!

So, next year? Well, we will start in early February. To be advised, of course. Stay tuned, guys. My turn for honouring.

Don't forget New Year's at Coolum/Peregian RSL. Also Morgan's house party on Dec 12.

Book of the night: *The Life You Were Born to LIVE* ... Dan Millman.

Merry Christmas and Happy New Year.

Dave of Maroochydore.

2010

Scott's Shed Feb 23, 2010

The second meeting of the year 2010 and we had a full attendance. Scott, Matt, Morgan, Roger, Greg and myself. Good to see that there are challenges and lessons learned in our check-ins. It's all good and it shows we are still learning and remaining open.

Scott looked after us with food and refreshments and also kept the mozzies at bay via a circle of burning repellents. Matt and I sprayed ourselves thoroughly on arrival and I think the aura of that fumigation helped also.

I was very humbled to be honoured tonight. And I shall be reading the words before I sleep tonight so my spirit is reminded of its good work. Thank you, guys! On that note, if you have your words on computer can you send via email for my records?

We had no actual topic but went over last meet's subject of teenagers. There just seems to be a struggle with communication. Two items that struck a chord for me were to make a special outing with each child to help in interaction (suggested by Scott). And to take the kids to an evening talk about car safety usually done by an organisation like the police. Car safety seeming to be a major topic with us all.

Greg let it be known that his life may be shifting away from this group. That's a loss for us but good that he can go with what he feels is right. Good journey, mate!

On Sat 20th and Sun 21st March we will be going camping. Men and boys only. With any luck we'll canoe down the Mary River and camp along its banks.

Next meeting at Roger's. That's Tuesday March 9. Morgan and myself will not be attending.

May I end with saying that this group is just so special, so important, and so unique. Thank you, men!

Dave of us.

Dave's Place April 13, 2010

Yes, I had the meeting at my place tonight. All were present. We total a number of five: Matt, Morgan, Scott, Roger and I. Check-in went for a longer time tonight. Each man had quite a bit to say and this led into further discussion. I chose the topic of 'desire' as mine seems to have evaded me lately. But after my check-in the guys talked about what was affecting me the most: guilt and grief.

Which basically are the opposites of desire.

Matt and I are separated from our long-time partners. So we seem to have a similar relationship situation and it can really tear you emotionally apart. Knowing you've done the right thing for the family's mental health but also realising that your family will never be the same. That connectedness is gone. There is a 'guilt' emotion that won't let you go. It suppresses the drive of 'desire'. Once that drive is not felt then the reason for even getting out of bed in the morning doesn't eventuate. You lose purpose, action, feelings, and your emotions are numbed.

The guys helped me realise that this is okay. That guilt and grief are to be observed for what they are. Experience them and go with the process. That's life.

I thank all the men for their help tonight. I have even forgiven myself of guilt because the focus was on me, not the group as a whole. Morgan said, "If we can't help a group member who is in trouble then what's the point of the group?" Scott's quote: "We can only row with the oars we have" rang true. Roger even broke into song about being open and closed which really capped the night off.

Matt stayed back and talked some more and I really appreciate that. I am just so thankful for our group. Guys, you are so much help. I honour you all.

Dave of less guilt.

Morgan's Place April 27, 2010

A significant date as Morgan's wife Hayley has finally decided to pursue her gift of 'channelling' or 'clairvoyance' and use this to pursue the greater good. From this small beginning she has now travelled all over the world to give readings. We are so fortunate that she gives us another aspect with our meetings.

Morgan had a special meeting planned for us tonight.

Present were Roger, Matt and myself. Scott had a meeting so came later on. During check-in it was interesting to me to see that our group is reading. Not that we had stopped at any stage but by reading we are expanding our knowledge and understanding of the life we live.

Manshine is knocking on the door again and I'm happy that Morgan and Roger are going. Such good memories of the first time I went. An almost enlightening experience. Can't wait to hear the stories upon their return.

Morgan presented us with a couple of DVDs: *The shadow Effect* and *Ambition to Meaning*. Looking forward to watching those as with everything in my life they will hold a strong message.

But that was only the beginning as Morgan's wife Hayley held a meditation for us. Hayley is so connected with spirit and we are fortunate that she wants to share that gift. With a background of Tibetan singing bowls she led us on a journey to talk with a higher spirit. And while we were deep in meditation she was busy writing up a reading for each of us. She read it to us and presented it at the end of the meditation.

Hayley then told us of a path she has been led to, to raise money for stolen and mistreated children from Cambodia. I have great admiration for her and I can see she is being led by a higher purpose for the greater good of us all. She is being spiritually led, which must be very gratifying to be able to see one's path so clearly.

Later Morgan asked the question, "Why do we come together to this men's group?" Answers such as to learn about ourselves, to speak up, to be open, being still, growth, awareness, all were discussed. This discussion led our group to talk about the spiritual or non-physical side that we sometimes experience. What is there? Will we ever really know? Do we need to know?

After checkout Hayley joined us to say goodbye. And as I left, I thought, can it get any better?

Hayley holds a meditation every Friday from 10 a.m. – 1 p.m.

Next meet at Matt's place.

Dave of M/Dore.

Matt's House Kings Beach May 11, 2010

All were present tonight. And 'present' we were during check-in as each man related to their last two weeks. I especially liked to hear about the Manshine experiences from Morgan and Roger. Roger in particular related to an interaction which moved him deeply. It makes me feel very excited when I hear of these stories. To see the men in our group actually connect with truth. And that truth has such a powerful reaction.

I also like to hear that the DVDs Morgan and Hayley gave out are having an impact on our kids. The message is getting out there. Speaking of 'messages', Scott was asking about the action of 'surrender' as mentioned in Wayne Dyer's DVD *Ambition to Meaning*. We discussed this at great length and eventually figured 'acceptance' was a better word.

Morgan suggested that we try an interaction used by his Common Ground group last week. And that was to pair up and ask each other "Who are you?" repeatedly; we did this for five minutes each. It gave us an insight as to who we are without our ego attached. I ended up saying that I was the feeling behind the thought. And I noticed that when I had eye contact with Roger I couldn't think of the answer. And Roger seemed to feel the same. Morgan paired up with Scott. Scott said he unfocused his eyes to give Morgan the answers.

Morgan also paired with Matt. And Matt came back to the table and announced to us what we had all known for some time. Out of the closet he came and about time too!

Speaking of which, I noticed we all had a few good belly laughs tonight. Such a good thing to do!

After checkout we discussed going to an area for some star gazing. This we must do as I intend to manifest some UFOs so one can land and take Roger and I back home!

Next meeting at Scott's and he's asked for 'straight' men only to attend!!! Just joking …

See you there HO.

Dave of Alfa Centauri.

Scott's Shed May 25, 2010

Present were Scott, Roger, Morgan and myself.

During check-in it seemed evident that there are changes in each man's life. Whereas the weather and seasons have definitely shifted, so has each man's personal circumstances. I find this very interesting. Is it a shift to follow the seasons, or a deeper shift inside one's own being? Has the change actually come from within? Merely to be reflected back to oneself?

153

Or a shift that is a natural occurrence which we are still not fully aware?

Roger announced that tonight is near enough for our two-year anniversary. That's two years since we finished Common Ground and wanted to keep the group going. If I recall correctly we had our first meeting at Cody's in Buderim.

Star gazing will definitely be on the menu at Scott's soon. He has a plan. So the first cloudless, moonless night we all agree on it will happen!

Rudolf Steiner was the subject on more than one occasion tonight. Scott will be heading a study group on one of his books, *How to Know Higher Worlds*, which sounds very interesting. Scott and Roger spoke of their experiences with the Steiner school concept. Their interaction with education as a whole interactive experience just sounds so beneficial.

We talked at some length about life purpose. And how a job becomes automatic but still has some intrigue left to create some enthusiasm.

Sarcasm (often quoted as the lowest form of wit) was discussed; it seems to be a mask or a defence used to cover inadequate self-reflection.

Sleep became another topic. I seemed to be the only man there who gets plenty. Roger, Morgan and Scott said that they tend to wake at 4 a.m. approximately with their brains buzzing. Worrying about things that have happened and will happen is a function of the left brain and the ego loves it. We all need a way to practise 'presence' and not feed this condition. Good sleep is essential to good health.

Another very good meeting. Thanks, Scott.

Next one at Roger's place HO!

Dave of presence … sometimes!

Roger's Place June 8, 2010

Meeting tonight at Roger's. Scott, Roger and Morgan. Sat round a fire in the rain with umbrellas up—eating fruit cake and sipping lemon tea! Loved it!

Discussion covered variety of topics, including careers, parenting and Mr Steiner. It's interesting how different our lives are on one level—but the commonality of our experiences is also evident. It's that shared experience that helps bind us and keep our group meaningful. Long may it last!

Next meeting down south—maybe at Dave's? Dave to confirm.

Ho, Morgan.

Dave's Place June 22, 2010

Three of us tonight at my place. Morgan, Scott and yours truly.

The night was advertised as Davo's Pizza Emporium.

I had two pizzas ready to go but Roger and Matt couldn't make it and Scott has an issue with gluten, so Morgan and I indulged ourselves. It's a bit hard to find gluten-free pizzas; I did go to Woolies under instruction but still couldn't find any. I missed Roger's last meeting and the guys remarked that it was just brilliant!

Upon check-in it was clear to see that we all have an issue with being present. We seem to lose it when a number of circumstances accumulate and we are presented with a situation in which we must react. Usually in the heat of the moment, and the end result was the same as if we hadn't tried at all … well, almost.

It would be good if we had a trigger, an alarm that registers in our minds to say, "Wait a minute, this outcome is going to be the same as last time, maybe I should take five, feel my breath, become present, before reacting."

Morgan mentioned counting to 10, letting your mind relax somewhat before the decision. Scott suggested leaving the response for a day or as long as possible so the heat comes out of the altercation. Take the anxiety out of the decision. I have practised not reacting with the ego, by giving a limited response, thereby giving no ammunition for the other person to react to. But unknown to me there has been a residue left in my body, manifesting as a backache. So I need to learn a way of dropping this from my body totally.

Scott and Morgan have been watching the soccer. Late nights prevail. And the umpire's decisions have been pretty poor. But when you are talking the World Cup, what's new?

I can see the attraction with this and many other major sporting events. The attraction is seeing it as it happens. You are actually very present and keenly focused as are many others at that same moment in time. So many spirits/consciousnesses at the one event, a moment when all are at one with each other.

We discussed how our partners viewed this group. And came to the conclusion that if you have a relationship problem, well, it'll show up as a generally suspicious view held by your partner. Usually they think of us whingeing about women, whereas in reality they are rarely the subject.

It's a half moon at the moment so I'll have to familiarise myself with the lunar calendar to figure out the best day for our night sky viewing. This'll be held at Scott's.

A camping date around the end of July would be good too. Scott suggested Inskip Point; he'll bring his boat. Would be great sitting around a fire cooking fresh fish via one of Jamie Oliver's frypans courtesy of Morgan. All past members are to be invited if we can contact them. So just putting it out there!

Next meet at MATT'S … and he doesn't even know it yet!

Scott's Place July 13, 2010

The 'Fantastic Four' were present. Brother Matt will be back soon, we hope.

The plan at Scott's was to have a check-in and then we would stargaze the rest of the night. Which we did in essence, but along the way we hit on so many subjects I can't remember them all.

Scott did ask that we contemplate our role in this cosmos, this universe we exist in. That subject was almost as unanswerable as 'Who am I?'

Check-in had a common thread as there seems to be more money leaving our collective households than coming in. And that is repeated in the wider community as reflected by the local media in tonight's TV. Many shops are shutting their doors and walking away. Not even making enough money to pay the rent! Mostly Mum-and-Dad businesses. Everyone is feeling the pinch. Morgan remarked that the average household bills are $350 more per month than this time last year. That is a staggering amount!

I did see a special report on the news about Port-au-Prince in Haiti. There are still a million people living in tents in that city. It's been six months since 230K people died and 300K were injured in that devastating earthquake. I

159

find that hard to imagine. We still have so much to be thankful for.

Scott, Roger and Morgan lay on rollout beds while I brought my own deckchair to watch the sky. Scott even provided blankets and if I didn't have a home to go to I'd still be there. It was very comfortable. We were rewarded with a cloudless night. Among the many stars we spotted three planes and at least as many small meteorites entering our atmosphere. Unfortunately, no UFOs … Maybe on the weekend we'll see them.

Speaking of which, it's all go for Inskip Point Saturday and night; should be great.

Just need a volunteer for our next meeting. HO! … Dave of Maroochydore

Boolumba Creek July 21, 2010

Well, it eventually happened. After two years of planning we finally had a camping trip together. Boolumba Creek!

Morgan 'Master of Ceremonies' (MC) transported Scott and Roger and also brought most of the food. I drove up separately with Matt 'Horny Goat' (HG) as we intended not to stay the night.

When we arrived Roger and Scott stripped down and jumped in the creek. Very brave! Then the group all sat around our campsite for a drink and chat. Later on we decided some exercise was needed and settled for the Gold Mine track 1.6 kms away. This was an easy walk and most enjoyable as each man took it at his own pace.

When we returned a beaut fire was made, (Roger supplied the firewood) and MC cooked us dinner. As darkness fell the stories began to flow.

Scott suggested that we consider where we will be in five and 10 years' time for a topic. The replies were fairly deep as each man tried to foretell his future. The strange thing about the topic for me was this is exactly what I have been staring down with the last few months.

Let's hope at the very least we still have this group in five or 10 years from now. I for one find it very valuable.

HG and I left about 10.30 p.m. so we missed all the snoring.

Thank you to everyone for making this happen.

HO ... Dave of Hope.

Morgan's Place July 27, 2010

A wet night received us for the meeting at Morgan's house. All were present and as always Morgan had something special prepared for us.

After check-in Hayley led us through a meditation and then presented us with a written page from our spiritual contacts.

Morgan had his mother contact him; Roger, his son; Scott, a distant relative; Matt, a relative named Phil; and my father tried talking some sense to me. We all appreciate Hayley for taking the time to do this for us.

After tea break we discussed dreams and how they are influencing us. Are they a message or just a reflection of what we already know? Perhaps the truth is not the dream but how we feel when we wake up, as Roger suggested.

Morgan asked what it is that keeps our group of five together. Answers such as privacy, friendship, unloading of mind talk, understanding, genuine concern and comfort all were discussed. How lucky are we to have such meetings that are this diverse?

Ho ... Next meet at HG's Sacred Shed!

Dave of the Rainstorm Coast!

HG's (Matt's) Penthouse Aug 10, 2010

Very heavy rain set in outside as we had our latest meeting. Present were HG, MC, Scott and myself.

Our host Matt (HG) invited us into his penthouse, and later told stories that could have come from that very magazine!

A common theme from check-in seemed to be each man had a midlife crisis. Maybe that word crisis is too harsh. More like a challenge or hurdle has been presented and we are being dared to take it on. The regimented life we all lead is also under question. Do we just keep maintaining the status quo or do we branch out to seek real inspiration?

Is this inspiration found, as HG discovered, in the bush or at the very least away from our busy city and suburbia? Or are we looking at it right now, presented in various forms through other people who are not seeing clearly? Are they just really teachers, meant to be in our life to waken a different thought pattern?

As Morgan said, "Life without a purpose is a life that is empty." It's easy to drift along to a certain extent. A passion in one's life keeps the flame burning, keeps a focus.

It's important to have the right mental attitude too. Scott gave an excellent example of two teachers walking into a classroom, one with angry, depressive thoughts and another with happy, uplifting ones. Their thoughts were the only communication; no words were spoken. The students could feel the teacher's aura of mental thoughts. I work in a school part time and have observed this with some of the teachers there too.

The lesson, as in many books we have all read, is be careful of your thoughts. Or at the very least, observe your thoughts, be aware of what mental energy you are putting out there.

Morgan talked about, and I quote: "The treadmill of accumulation". How we are all consumers set in a pattern of consumption. If we leave the treadmill, we are accused of being abnormal or other words designed to make us feel guilty. Yet it is those very people who leave the treadmill, who branch out, who dare to be different that we all end up admiring!

A popular phrase at the moment is "Who or where is the elephant in the room?", meaning there is a large, overwhelming presence with us that we are not aware of.

I think the presence is consciousness, it's the elephant. We cannot see or feel it as we're lost in our own thoughts, mind noise … ego.

I made a conscious effort before I slept that night to be grateful for everything and everyone in my life. Even the person who made my bed. I slept for 12 hours.

Next meeting at my place, guys. Morgan can't make it due to work commitments.

HO … Dave of sleep.

Dave's Place Aug 24, 2010

There were four of us tonight at my place, as Morgan was away at work.

Matt and I had dinner before Scott and Roger arrived and we then all sat at the dining table having a cuppa, some nibbles and a brief chat.

Check-in provided no real lead for the night but that was okay as Scott had sent an idea via email during the last week. Scott has been having insomnia lately and during the long nights awake has been questioning what sort of message has been sent to him. He came to the conclusion that it may be 'desire'. Is he doing what he really desires? Then he thought it would make a great subject for our group.

Roger has a secret passion/desire and that seems to be (for want of a better explanation) blowing up things! And he presented quite an elaborate DVD that he and his brother made at Xmas 2005. It featured a vacuum cleaner sucking up petrol from a bucket. Which then caught fire and looked like an experimental jet engine for a while until the whole lot went up in flames. It was good to see that all workplace health and safety issues were addressed adequately. Well … Roger did have safety goggles on. Anyway, the name of this DVD is called *Funniest Home Myth Busters* and is available at all good retail outlets. And it's bloody funny!

Thanks for that, Roger!

I was feeling in a good space after that so I decided to take the plunge and read the foreword and first chapter of a book I've been writing called *Insanity Beach*. Surprisingly, no-one fell asleep and I even had some good feedback. But funnily, as I have never read it out loud, it seemed disjointed, and missing some flow. Anyway, it did feel good to get a bit of creativity out there.

So, guys, who is next?

I'm looking forward to hearing some of Scott's song writing next time. And HG's desires are too risqué to put on this family-friendly site but are eagerly sought by the rest of us.

So this will be good. Next meet at Roger's place. Bring something to blow up!

Ho, Dave of Desire. And 50 years old tomorrow!

The Creative Spark Sept 7, 2010

I'm sitting here trying to write anything near to justifying the night we just had … It was so packed with interesting topics and content. Everyone was there except HG and it was definitely a 'don't miss' night out!

The heading 'Roger's Place Sept 7, 2010' doesn't hint at anywhere near the experience I just had. Hence 'The Creative Spark' seems more apt.

Roger had everything prepared: tea, food and as always, a beaut fire.

During check-in I noticed that every man had a major event in the calendar just happen or about to happen, which is unique in itself. Roger mentioned he had recently done a dream workshop which led us all to discuss various dreams we have had. In particular, what these actual dreams mean, and how they relate to what is happening in real life.

Scott talked about how the creative process works through him to write songs. Then he sang one of his own works titled 'Shine On'. I thought it was brilliant. I kept picturing a movie scene in my head as the song seemed like it should be the main theme. Scott was inspired by a poem which also inspired Mandela to use it in his speech.

That wasn't all, as then we were treated by another song of Scott's titled 'Cody and the Angels of Love' which was professionally done on a CD. And as I'm writing this that song is still buzzing along in my head! This song came to Scott after he had his first experience with toning. And I hope at some time Scott can take us through that experience.

Intermission: And Morgan who is 44 tomorrow brought along his own birthday cake. And seeing as he missed my birthday last meeting we both shared the celebrations.

The next item on the night's agenda needs its own title!

Roger's Fire

You've heard of St Elmo's Fire; well, Roger's Fire eats that. He can create flames from water!

Roger led us down the garden path, so to speak, and I was worried that any moment something near us would burst into flames. But we all arrived safely near his backyard frog pond/dam and sat down.

He then walked to the opposite side of the dam and lit his eternal flame. I thought it was on the bank until after arriving back he asked me to pull a string attached to a hand reel. As I did this I noticed the flame coming closer so realised it was in a float of some sort. Roger then disappeared again and was busy turning something on in the bush not far from us. As he came back the floating flame which was now halfway across suddenly ignited a rather larger flame. It had a great effect on the water. I realised that he had a gas supply under the water as you could see it burbling up and it could also be smelt. But I have never seen that done before so was mightily impressed.

To top it off he had also rigged a water fountain to spray onto the flames, and so from that moment on 'Riverfire of Brisbane' was destined to always be the second fiddle!

It's going to be very hard to top that night. Well done, guys! Next meet at Morgan's: Roger will be away following HG's lead …

Dave of indecision.

Morgan's Place Sept 21, 2010

And then there were three.

Yes, a small group at this meeting: Morgan our host, Scott and me.

After check-in it was Morgan's turn to introduce his passion. And it was for the 'Swannies', the Swans Football club. His story unfolded from when he was a young boy living near Perth, WA. He had an enthusiasm for watching TV sport which wasn't understood by the rest of his family. He told how he'd watch cricket and use a calculator to work out their run rates. But footy was his love. At age 12 he'd travel many kilometres on the weekend just to watch his favourite club play a live game. This addiction followed him to Sydney where he became attached to the Sydney Swans.

He showed us a DVD of the Grand Final in 2005. Swans vs. Eagles. Considered as one of the greatest games in sporting history in this country. We only watched the last five minutes but I could feel the tension portrayed by the crowd. It had been 72 years since they had won a grand final!

Morgan's obsession even follows him to bed. He cures insomnia by going over all the players and their positions on the oval inside his head. By centre half forward he'll usually drop off to sleep. Morgan's a passionate follower.

I think it was Tolle who said that watching sport helps us focus, and can bring us physically and emotionally into the present. It's good for the soul to be held in the present. Even better to watch a live game and feel the presence of the entire crowd around us.

Thanks, Morgan.

Morgan then presented us Steve Biddulph's book *The New Manhood*. We discussed the five awakenings. They are: You are going to die; Life is hard; You are not that important; Your life is not about you; You are not in control of the outcome.

In other words, Life Sucks, Get Over it! And I know why I turned up after that discussion as I have been in a 'hole' the last week! So Morgan's off to Paris, Scott to Borneo and Roger is already in Carnarvon Gorge. So we expect picture presentations and an interesting talk from you three when we meet again.

And the meeting will be at Matt's Shack on October 26. That's what happens if you're not there! Morgan has a Xmas party on Dec 18 and has invited us. Thanks, mate.

Ho to everyone, Dave.

Dave's Place Nov 2, 2010

Three people at my place tonight: Morgan, Roger and I. Matt is probably in Victoria and Scott has returned from Borneo with an unwelcome bug!

We each had a fairly long check-in as it has been many weeks since we last met. Roger had a good time at Carnarvon Gorge and Morgan enjoyed himself in Paris and Scotland. I didn't go anywhere but enjoyed meeting people at various coffee shops around town.

We discussed holidays and how the planning/anticipation of such seem to almost be as good as the actual event. And I realised that another year has gone by without going on one myself. Must get to New Zealand next year.

The subject of patterns in your life and the connection to your emotional path was raised. How we are influenced by emotional conflict or damage by our parents and pass this onto future generations. Counselling seems a good way to cut this path or perhaps a recognition of the pattern can be just as beneficial.

This wrap-up is probably a bit short but I'd like to add one thing. It is just so good to have a meeting again.

I miss it and all you guys! Keep strong and see you at Scott's place in two weeks' time. Tuesday Nov 16.

HO ... Dave.

Scott's Symphony Nov 16, 2010

Matt could not come again tonight so present were Scott, Roger, Morgan, Phil and myself. It was Phil's first time and I would like to welcome him on behalf of all of us.

Let me describe the scene ... At ground level Scott had ignited a white man's fire with enough heat and radiation to power a small village! Above that was a silhouette of trees with a clouded canopy all lit by our sun's light bouncing off a half moon.

But it was the backing chorus that gave the night character. A symphony of various native frogs all competing for their own version of the *X Factor*!

Phil checked in first (very brave) and I could sense that here is a man who is searching or questioning life itself. A quest we are all familiar with. He'll fit in well and I and the other men will welcome his input.

After we all checked in we discussed presence. This topic keeps coming up and I feel we do not really have a good understanding of it. It may be good to do a brief meditation each meeting just to remind us all what it feels like to be 'present'.

Three other topics were raised: observation, control and responsibility.

Observation of our thoughts is a clear indication that we are separating the ego from our spirit or being. The one thing that prevents us from what we think we are to what we actually are. And what is that? Well, I believe we are one. All collected in consciousness.

Does that mean you have to agree? No, not at all …

Control and responsibility seemed to cross over to some extent. Particularly when Scott was talking about the Borneo trip and how he was responsible for all these teenagers but had no control of the situation they were all in. I could understand the 'fear' this would generate. As men we all have this inbuilt into our psyche. But is this just a lesson to let go? Can you really have complete control over any situation? If true, then should you allow yourself the burden of the responsibility associated with that?

Or is it all a metaphor for life itself? Why did that situation get attracted into my life and if it keeps occurring then there may be an emotion that has not been dealt with? Can you really let go so you don't worry, don't stress? Are we taking responsibility away from the individuals who need to learn the lesson the most? And by doing that are we setting them up for a greater fall when that lesson finally comes home to roost?

These questions we will ponder till our next meeting. This will be at Roger's place on Nov 30. HO, guys! Dave of M/Dore.

Roger's Place Nov 30, 2010

Present were Morgan, Scott, Phil, Matt, myself (Dave), and of course Roger.

It's always interesting at Roger's place. Maybe it's the 'mechanic' in me that notices the different machines and tools. Roger had a unique nut cracker that we used on his macadamias. And the centre table display had an anvil made from a railway track, with the talking stick represented by a homemade chipping hammer. Both being the property of a deceased friend. Even as we left I was impressed by the engineering used on a lady's bike under the pergola.

Check-in was interesting as always but more so as it seemed to merge into the main discussion. There seemed no point where there was any cut-off separating the two.

Each man was talking about 'turning points' in their lives. And the effect his 'decisions' made from that point onwards. It seems that the 'laws of attraction' have such a great effect on everything. Especially in the field of affection and love.

Kids were the focal point too. At what point do you draw the line and stop just giving them what they want? Will handing over the responsibility for what they want to them force a realisation inside our kids that for each action there has to be an equal or opposite one? Kids start young wanting as society dictates an accumulation of 'things'. To be good consumers! Perfect for ego attachment, really! The want for something more or better. The ego can then identify itself as missing out or rejected. So the ego then looks for the person responsible for this feeling, the weakest parent. I think we have to ask, "Who's the boss here?"

Rites of passage for teens was another topic. For all cultures within Australia, even our Aboriginals, it all centres on alcohol. Be interesting if alcohol was taken out of the equation.

Even drink driving which can end in fatality has been experienced within our group. How can we discourage this practice? Maybe getting the drivers to experience a real-life film of a fatal accident with nothing cut out would create a realisation?

Phil asked about the turning point in a relationship. At what point do you sacrifice yourself or the kids? Do you carry on even when the relationship is over just for the kids' sakes?

Such a hard decision which is exactly what it's meant to be. The internal 'pain bodies' of each adult lie exposed and can't be repaired by their partner. The blame will cascade back and forward until one gives in. The ego loves this stuff, thrives on it, in fact. Always focusing inward and blaming others for its feelings. But the feelings are actually being allowed by the person to happen inside their head. No-one has forced this upon them. Expose the feeling or emotion, look at it, accept it. Don't blame another person for its existence. The moment you do this it loses power. It doesn't attract the conflict it enjoys feeding off. The conflict then cannot be reflected by others around you.

There seemed to be a cycle that we witnessed tonight. It was Frustration – Anger – Reasonability! Look at the cycle; shine a light of realisation on it!

Checkout was a combination of jokes and quotes.

Roger said; "Scott is a glow worm struggling on the hook of time."

Phil said; "If you're going to eat an elephant start at the tail."

Scott's joke: A bloke goes overseas for six months and gets his brother to look after his cat. Three days before his return he rings up to ask how the cat is going. "He's dead!" said the brother. "Well," said the bloke, "you could have broken it to me more gently. Like you could have said that the cat got stuck in a tree, we called the fire brigade. They came around and unfortunately the cat fell down and died." "Oh, okay," said his brother. "Anyway," the bloke said, "how's Mum?" "Well," said his brother, "Mum got stuck up a tree, we called the fire brigade, unfortunately …"

Next meeting at Matt's on Tuesday December 14. Morgan won't be there and Dave by phone from Vic. HO, guys! Dave of M/Dore.

Matt's Shed Dec 14, 2010

Present were Scott, Roger, Phil, Les, and of course Matt. Morgan was working in Sydney and Dave in Melbourne. Dave did a check-in via phone. This was also Les's first meeting and we welcome him for his valuable contribution.

Apparently the discussions centred on relationships, including anger, growth, learning and various levels of personal development.

Scott added that the food was good, although he mentioned that there was a vast gap of unconsciousness between when he scaled the spiral staircase 'at the entrance' to when he walked back down it to leave. He did notice that Roger left with a piano accordion though!

Scott and Matt gave this thorough update to me so an account can be kept on our progress within the group.

HO, Dave.

2011

Dave's place Feb 1, 2011

Present was a full house! Matt, Roger, Morgan, Phil, Les, Scott and myself.

Pizza and garlic bread was on the menu.

During check-in it was interesting to hear about each man's experiences over the Xmas and New Year period. This time of year is always a challenge for relationships, as pressures of work, money and parenting over the holiday period have a large effect. Roger talked about heart transplants and how this organ seems to have a memory that affects its new owner. Phil is tackling *The Power of Now*, a book which for me was a major turning point in my life.

Scott checked in last and a topic appeared after he asked for input on a fear-related subject. How do we convey our concerns to our kids, particularly teenagers, without conveying our 'fears' to them? Do we just not say anything so as to keep the law of attraction at bay? Or will we attract that scenario anyway because of our fears? What age do our kids stop holding respect for our opinions? Will they learn from us or will they just have to learn by experience? How do you teach self-discipline or consequences from your actions without actually experiencing them with some sort of feeling or emotion attached?

We will be having much more discussion on this subject!

After tea-and-cake break Roger played us a tune on the accordion that Matt had lent him from the last meeting. He did a great job restoring what at best was an instrument well past its prime. He asked us to close our eyes and listen. The tune 'did it' for me and he obviously had some affinity with it. I think he is very talented! Great way to end the meeting.

The accordion was then passed to Matt and it's his job to play a tune next meeting. Then it will be my turn!

And the next meeting will be at Morgan's place. Feb 15, 2011.

Thanks guys … HO HO. Dave.

Morgan's Place Feb 15, 2011

Tonight's meeting was at Morgan's place and usually that means the special bonus of a reading from Hayley.

A full house in attendance too, I hope this will be the norm from now on. There is just so much more input when we have seven men.

Check-in took quite a while. It was evident that most of us had experienced 'anger' in the last two weeks. An unpleasant emotion which can really attract unpleasant reactions especially when egos are aroused. Stress and communication are really big issues for us as well. But I am pleased that we can recognise these emotions/issues within ourselves which shows a high degree of personal development.

Valentine's Day (yesterday) got a mention too. It was interesting to hear each man's viewpoint on this day in respect to how he handles it. Which unfortunately we only touched on at the end of our meeting.

After check-in we started a discussion on enneagrams: these are used to find out what type of personality we are. Phil said that there is an online test that you can take which would be interesting. I remember doing a personality test many years ago on the four basic types: Sanguine, Choleric, Phlegmatic and Melancholy. I recall that there is a book about this subject called *Personality Plus*; well worth a read. Another book called *The Life You Were Born to Live* by Dan Millman is an excellent 'ice breaker' or coffee-table book to get a handle on a person's purpose.

Anyway, the clock was ticking ever faster and we were just getting into some interesting discussion when Morgan reminded us that Hayley was going to do a meditation and reading this evening. I find it quite interesting to see what the 'spirits' are saying to us. And it also says a lot about your state of mind at the time of the meditation.

By now it was quite late and unfortunately we had to leave. So I hope we can gather up where we left off when we meet again at Matt's place on March 1.

Thank you, Morgan and Hayley for making that such an excellent meet.

HO, Dave.

Matt's New Place March 1, 2011

Matt has moved house and what a beautiful new house it is! The balcony where we held the meeting just had a perfect breeze and temperature, considering that the daylight hours saw around 34 degrees.

Nearly all men were present and indeed 'presence' was discussed greatly during this meeting. We were only missing Scott who now pays the price of holding the next one!

Check-in for most of us seemed to be about deadlines. Either work or relationship driven, as we all seemed to have an important issue looming. We also discussed the basic rules of our 'leaderless' men's group and I will endeavour to get those in print.

It was an interesting observation that Phil discussed when referring to the natural disasters happening in our world this year. That it brings us back to basics, strips away our attachment to 'things', or 'form', as Tolle would put it. And what is left? The basic human needs! Compassion, humility, love and a real sense of the common bond between all humans. A sense of community again, of concern for each other. We all hope this consciousness will last as Les commented, before we revert back to the norm. Or can that be, after experiencing a life-changing event on such a scale as our state has done? Even our much—for want of a better word—'hated' premier has shown the human, compassionate side that is within her. And her maligned people have responded with a real boost to her opinion polls.

Phil has just finished *The Power of Now* by Eckhart Tolle. And we have all had an experience with this book. So good to see it has switched some lights on. Most people who read it just find it so enlightening but it can also repel others. What does this mean? It means that this book can be a part or not a part of someone's journey.

What I personally like to hear is if the reading of this book or any other brings a brief realisation of true enlightenment. And what is that? Well, you'll know when it happens.

Phil also put forward a discussion on relationships. At what point do you know when there is nothing left or anything to save? If you are moving in different directions and communication is woeful: is that a sign? Or is it just an ego battlefield? The truth I believe is that it's a sign that you need help. From the group and also professionally. But the overall sign is the simple fact that we are men seeking answers. And our presence in this group will open our minds to the answers we need. The fact that we are in this group boldly shows me that we are all heading in the right direction. And that direction? It's within!

I have written this many times and I suppose it's worth saying it again. The simple fact that we observe what we are thinking puts us one step ahead of an ego-led decision. Observation of thought is like shining a light into a black cave. The light exposes the thought to question, not as it is right or wrong, but its hidden source.

As Morgan said and Matt agreed, you are meant to be happy. Life is not about torture! Sure, someone can torture you but do you have to torture yourself? Trust yourself, truth and reality will be shown to each and every one of us. Just make sure your mind is open when it's presented.

Next meet at Scott's ... I think! March15.

Scott's Place March 15, 2011

We welcome another full house, great to see, guys!

Scott's place is always special as we can enjoy the feeling of raw earth beneath our shoes, hear various nocturnal animal sounds and gaze at a roaring white man's fire! And tonight have the 2/3 moon overhead to reflect some ambient light ... Beautiful ...

During check-in Morgan introduced a talking stick to the group. A modern artefact made in the tradition of the Cherokee Indians. A fine piece of natural wood decorated with feathers on top, fur in the middle and snake skin on the bottom. It also has painted images of a scorpion, chameleon and a shell. Thanks, mate!

Our check-in was a mixture as always. Some men having real success at work while others still seeking direction for that achievement. Books were mentioned, great to hear that we are reading too. A book that you are drawn to read can often have some real enlightening messages in it.

Scott had mentioned 'toning' in the past to our group and tonight he felt it was right to start. We began by chanting/ groaning the 'Ohm'. Scott said that if you can 'groan' you can 'tone'. And he was right as we experienced some real harmonic synchronicity and it felt very comfortable. Next we picked a member of the group to tone to. Basically singing his name and sending the energy which he requested.

The recipient reported that he felt a release of stress, a type of surrender. And that he felt the energy pushed to him from us. We have decided to do each member in turn from now on.

Meditation was talked about over tea break and this will be done before check-in at all our subsequent meetings. We also talked about these write-ups and agreed that no names be mentioned. But I have taken a liberty by mentioning names again, as I believe that the context written is not of a personal nature. I hope that sits well?

Next meeting at my place so I get to house the talking stick until then. Les has offered to bring a large singing bowl for meditation so that will be a real treat!

HO, guys. Thanks, Dave.

Les's Place April 12, 2011

Present were of course Les, Scott, Roger and yours truly. Apologies from Morgan at work, also Phil and Matt who are having some chill time.

It was our first meeting at Les's and what a beautiful place he has. It felt very inviting and his background choice of music, 'Holy Harmony', set us in a good mood for the night.

We actually talked quite a lot in the kitchen when we arrived and this virtually became a part of check-in.

Eventually we sat down for our real check-in and I did a basic meditation to get us settled. Check- in was varied as always but dreams and spiritual insights did get a mention. Other right-brain activity such as toning and drawing raised themselves too. Even Facebook reared its head and was discussed later in length.

Many topics entered the arena tonight.

Drawing things as they are seen by shading/colour rather than by shape, and also the way Da Vinci could see movement and show that on paper.

Water levels and predictions of an 800 mm rise by century's end, and the implications to real estate in our immediate area.

Solar panels and the way they can benefit a household's power bill. The implications of insurance and future power needs. Are they as cost effective in their price versus the same amount invested at 6% over the term of approximately 25 years?

As mentioned, Facebook was talked about and its role in society. Is it a friend or foe? Is it used to replace physical interaction? Is that a good or bad thing? Or is it just another waste of time in cyberspace?

Books got a look in and I'm thankful to now know of *The Body is the Barometer of the Soul* which I shall be purchasing soon.

Thank you, Les and all the guys for this meeting. Next one is at Roger's on May 3 unless that isn't convenient.

HO, guys, Dave.

Roger's Sacred Site April 17, 2011

'Be prepared' seems to be Roger's motto as whatever the meeting had in store he was already on it! A 'full house' tonight, I'm glad to write, and we were greeted with a very ambitious white man's fire. It was so well structured that had we some old iron ore, an anvil and a mash hammer we could have forged some excellent swords.

The atmosphere was quite unusual as we had a very bright full moon and a fair amount of cumulous cloud. Just when we were settled for check-in it rained: a moon shower? Roger sprang up and within a minute we each had a man-sized umbrella to shelter under. Because of the rain noise I announced it would be good to meditate to as we were all standing and looking into the fire. About 10 minutes later the rain passed and check-in started again.

Interesting to hear each man's story tonight. The common threads were work stress, relationships, paradigm shifts, curve balls and depression. There's a quote of mine but I guess I wasn't the first to use it. "If everything is going well in your life then you obviously haven't a clue what's really going on."

Yes, sarcastic, I know, but I could see merit in that phrase tonight. It seems like as soon as the ego kicks in then a natural path gets kicked out. In stressful situations the 'spirit' in each of us just dissolves and we are left naked, fully exposed to the ego. Depression is another mind pool that the ego loves to bathe in. Focusing inwards can be a revelation to the spirit but the ego unfortunately wants it all his way.

Sometimes a sudden 'paradigm shift' happens along to pull you back to reality, but underlying emotional triggers and unlearnt lessons will always stop that being the norm.

Note that each man considered escaping into the bush as a natural way to reconnect with himself. Reconnecting with nature or a natural state of being.

Phil's poetic descriptions of Roger's gardens, I quote: Beautiful energy of the gardens and the majesty of the ancient grass tree beside us capped off the check-in. We had a brief discussion of society pressures and stereotypes in relation to the disparity of income between partners, before the rain came down again. There was an adaptive shift with this shower and we broke off into smaller groups. These smaller groups made it easier to be heard and the subjects were quite different. As quoted: The rain produced fractional splitting into pairs, each spouting irrelevant gossip!

Manshine is upon us again and one of the presenters, Andrew Barnes, is a qualified sexual educator and is in touch with the ups and downs of male sexuality. According to one video seen he can make a woman orgasm without touch. Maybe you prefer the old-fashioned way? Well, it does sound very interesting.

Not privy to most of the discussions I can say that Phil and I had a good chat about consciousness. That pure conscious thought and presence is probably far beyond the reach of mere mortal men. And 'truth' as an absolute is probably a word which doesn't fit its own meaning. This and much more will be discussed next time at my place on May 31.

Don't forget the camp date is closing on July 23, Bulimba Creek.

Till next fortnight … HO!

Dave the Planker.

Dave's Place June 8, 2011

Almost a full house tonight with the exception of Phil. It has been three weeks since the last meeting as most of us had problems with the last date.

As we ate and drank around the table Les gave us all a gift voucher for 'Trinfinity 8'. His wife Cheryl runs a rejuvenation and restoration system that uses Algorithmic Revitalisation Technology. Wow, that will certainly sort us out! Thank you, Les and Cheryl!

We usually now start with a meditation but instead this time we did a 'toning'. Firstly, we turned off the electric lights and stood in a small circle, the only ambient light supplied by a small candle placed on the coffee table. We started with a group "Ohm" and stopped after a few minutes then invited anyone to the centre to be 'toned'.

I went first followed by another member; we each held the candle in our hands while standing in the centre of the group circle. Each man has a unique experience with toning and our brother asked for 'Clarity'; he said he tried to focus and enjoyed the experience.

I wanted inner 'peace', a release from anger. A first time for me and such a unique experience. I was standing still with my eyes closed but my mind instantly fired up. Flashes of light and rumbling sounds were racing into my mind. It was chaos in there! It was as though someone or something was pulling impulses/thoughts out from my mind and not wanting to go they then raced back in. Like a boxing match in a minefield, at one stage I could feel deep sadness and my eyes filled with tears. I was trying to calm down but this went on for about half of the elapsed time. The second half, peace finally entered my head. I could relax and enjoy the resonance of the

195

voices surrounding me. Interesting to hear we have the tenor of Scott balanced by the baritone of Morgan, with the rest of us filling in between. Scott did say later that he could feel that I wasn't connecting early on so that shows the conscious melding that is experienced.

The Toning probably lasted most of the night. In fact, we had a tea break straight afterwards as it was getting late.

Stories of great elation to outright slander showed how varied we are. Good to see some men actually moving on with their lives in particular as regards to employment. Employment or 'work' was as always a major topic. Let's face it, it involves so much of our time, the least we can expect is that it's for the most part enjoyable. Or maybe it belongs in the same box as most other four letter words!

We probably experienced one of the briefest check-ins ever tonight. With, and I quote, "I'm good", and later when our brother was asked to elaborate he replied, "Still good" …

Scott left us with a riddle that I have been pondering.

What am I?

Greater than God
More evil than the Devil
Poor have it
Rich need it
Eat it and you'll die

I'm guessing and going out on a limb here that the answer is "nothing" but I stand to be corrected on this. I just thought of one … What's the gift of intuition … answer: realisation?

Next meeting Morgan's Place on June 21.

HO, guys and thank you.

Dave … ohm …

Scott's Place June 21 2011

Tonight a full house
The bush setting ensured
A gathering of men whose voices endured.
First in song of acceptance and then some space
To gathering thoughts from many a place
Seven tales told one at a time
Check-in was long but no-one would mind.
One needed love
One needed to let go
One was anxious about the new show
One was being taught on what he attracted

197

The other doubted that his attraction was manufactured.

One had faith in what he had chosen

The last chose to conceive that his mind remains open.

All of these men will gather again

On the 5th of July at Morgan Haslup's domain.

Morgan's Place July 5, 2011

Five men strong tonight, missing Matt and Les.

We all started with a cuppa and I must admit I was quite attracted to Morgan's orange cake. Eating it didn't disappoint and I for one couldn't believe how moist it was. How could something so moist be born in an oven at probably 180 degrees for 30 minutes?

Check-in was a mixture of emotions from pain to elation. Frustration and oversensitivity also entered the conversations. We all received a gift from Scott as he had produced another nine songs on CDs titled 'Another 9 Songs' for us all.

A discussion about relationships came from check-in and continued to hold our attention for quite some time. At what point does it get uncomfortable enough to make changes in communication techniques? Or does that point only 'happen' when the two people involved can see clearly enough within themselves?

Morgan then held a 'forgiveness meditation' which was a great benefit to us all.

Thanks, Morgan, as yet again you have chaired a great meeting.

See you all in three weeks at my place on July 26, 2011.

HO. Dave.

Dave's Place July 26, 2011

It's been three weeks since the majority of us last met. With Les even longer as he had a two-week holiday in Cairns. Phil and Matt were indisposed and we missed their input.

I had a pumpkin soup brewing and it really hit the spot going by the comments and that set us up for check-in.

The theme running through check-in seemed to be presence, or the lack of it. That then affected us in various emotional ways. The elation of becoming present seems to alter those around us too, bringing them into the same state of consciousness. Then there is the reverse effect of holding on to our past disappointments. This holds people around us in that same state of consciousness, or as Tolle describes it, unconsciousness. But then it's really not that simple because an emotion held by an individual is continually broadcast outwards even if it's not realised. More present animals can pick up on this, such as pets. My dog, for example, will run to my aid if I am watching a TV show that triggers an emotion.

The main discussion centred on the 'restorative chat' card in Scott's possession. It basically outlined a number of written steps to help persuade your children to take responsibility for their actions. This is it in detail.

To the Wrong Doer

We're here to talk about ...

What were you thinking at the time?

What have you thought about since?

Who do you think has been affected by what you did?

What do you need to make things right?

How can we make sure this doesn't happen again?

What can I do to help you?

To the Victim

What did you think when it happened?

What have you thought about since?
How has it affected you?
What's been the worst of it?
What's needed to make things right?
How can we make sure this doesn't happen again?

When Stuck

Was it the right or wrong thing to do?
Was it fair or unfair?
What exactly are you sorry for?
You didn't answer my question.

Les then led a discussion about EMFs (electromotive force) and their potential damage to living things, most predominantly us. Whilst listening I was noting how many sources I had in my house with the fluoro lights, fridge motor and the sound system quietly playing behind us, it being operated by my iPhone which is an apparent large emitter, that is always by my side. As in Joe Jackson's song 'Everything Gives You Cancer', I wonder if there is anything produced by humans that doesn't give you that?

Even emotional damage can be claimed as carcinogenic!

Scott's place in two weeks unless it's raining, then it'll be Roger's.

HO, guys.

Dave.

Dave's Place Sept 6, 2011

A shaky start to the night as there was confusion as to whether there was an actual meeting and exactly where it was. Luckily we all ended up at my house minus Morgan and Matt. Morgan was away with work in Sydney and Matt was still battling the odds working way out west.

At check-in it was notable that we are all being confronted with issues that are designed to push our egos' buttons. We are forced to make a stand on behalf of our self-beliefs, the implications of which really put us into stress.

Can the solution be as easy as to just ask to be taken away from that position? Or is it a matter of focus? Are we concentrating on our own judgement as if this is the only way? Do we let others express their opinions about us? Does that in turn really tell us more about them? Can we maintain being the observer long enough to dig us out of a hole that others seem to have created? Or is it merely just another manifestation of our own thoughts projected into our daily lives creating the world in which we exist?

Two statements to give some thought.

1. I don't mind what happens.

2. Is it your shit or their shit and who is going to flush it?

We all missed out on the camp organised for last weekend. But instead of getting angry or upset about it we all agreed it worked out well. Each of us had something important to do and we just went with the flow. We'll try again on 15/16th October. Speaking of dates, don't forget Scott's anniversary on October 8, 2011.

We entered a discussion about lucid dreaming and found that some of us have the control of our dreams. By control I mean to interact with what is happening by being conscious. Acting like an observer or a puppeteer controlling the situation. Is that a point in reference to an almost spiritual existence whilst being unconscious? Or more an act of strong will?

Just as we were having a late tea break before checkout Matt checked in via phone. It was very informative to hear about the environment he's working in. And all the trials and tribulations he's subjected to.

Be strong, mate!

Next meeting at Morgan's on Sept 20, 2011.

HO, Dave.

Scott's Place Sept 20, 2011

An 'almost' black man's fire greeted Les, Roger and I at Scott's place tonight. Morgan was still working away so had to cancel.

We grabbed a tea each and some Anzac biscuits then sat down for a chat with a chorus of various frog noises in the background. The sky was clear and the temperature near perfect but lack of moon light left us in an opaque blackness. The odd mozzie interrupted my train of thought but personal Aerogard sorted him and his mates out.

Check-in was rather lengthy. It involved nostalgia, realisations and the general vulnerability of being a dad. I did note that we have very good understanding of what drives us, or in the opposite, what should be left alone. On that note can I announce "Scott the snake-handler"??

Afterwards we had a discussion about creativity and how that can be fostered without risking lifestyle. Creating something in your mind can be the fun bit. The reality of bringing it into action or form is the hard part. This can be harder if your income is totally consumed by the day-to-day workings of our society. Nothing left over to pursue any dreams. Roger pointed out that there is a growing consensus looking into this problem politically. It's a type of Basic Income Guarantee (German origin). Eliminating the dole but providing basic living standards. Helping to realise creativity without sacrifice would be very worthwhile.

Les told a story of how enthusiasm creates opportunity and how remaining 'open' can lead you down the right path to its fruition. That is something we all have experienced but I wonder if we actually realise when it is happening. Morgan has a quote that lends itself along these lines too.

Climate change, refugees and politics had a strong mention too.

I must say, Joey visited us a number of times during the night for a pat but Ellie also turned up, probably because all creatures great and small were attracted to our brief discussion of JC in his new hideout in Kingaroy.

Next meeting on Oct 4 at Roger's Place. HO, guys. Dave.

Roger's Place Oct 4, 2011 by Roger

Under the light of the half moon, it was the first trial of my new firepit, the black fellas would have been envious of the rich, deep, fiery-red coal bed, compared to their mulga scrub stick fires! All went well, extended casual check-ins; after about an hour of goss beforehand, I needed Morgan to keep the large unwieldy group on task and focused. There was a loose theme around travel and the richness that can be gained from such activities, then a very deep and intense communicative cohesive and cognoscenti on the finer art of kite boarding, while Phil was deeply entranced in the richness of the fire!

Also discussion around insulating one's self "not from the hot fire" but from negative media and enriching life through awareness of land and spirit, while being aware of ancient light shining on us from another time long past.

I came away from the night with renewed hope for humanity and my life.

Regards, Roger.

Scott's Place Nov 15, 2011

A dark night greeted us, highlighted by a multitude of stars. They would've been the focus if it wasn't for the brilliant white man's fire we faced. Throughout the evening, a background chorus of pond frogs would suddenly interject on occasion as they jockeyed for the strongest voice then just as suddenly fall silent. Phil informed us it was just 'chest beating'.

The two 'Ms' were missing … Morgan and Matt. We hope to all catch up next time.

Check-in produced a mixed bag of challenges and problems.

From sickness and depression to physical challenge and elation. Can we break up the mundane and somehow gain control? Or is control the very thing we don't need? How do we let go without losing, or are we supposed to lose? We seem to have so much on our collective plates. As Phil remarked it's like these 'plates' are on a lazy Susan; as soon as you've finished one another turns up to challenge you. Who's turning 'Susan' then? Consciousness, unconsciousness, god, fate, or someone/thing else?

What's the cure? Munching kale?

We then had varied discussion.

Two men have taken up the challenge of kite surfing. They have decided to try something that if suggested 20 years ago would have been thought to be nigh impossible. Controlling wind, waves, direction and body balance all at once seems quite a task to me but plenty of people do it and the sport is growing.

Interaction with our fathers was questioned. For all of us it is far different to our present family situation. Seems we were all faced with the façade of unemotional indifference that was the norm in the previous generation. As roles have changed so men have had to adapt and now share more responsibility for their children's upbringing. A good thing too.

We all generally agree that men have a real problem expressing themselves emotionally. How do we fix that? It seems to me that it belongs in the 'seek and ye shall find' basket. We are seekers and have found an outlet to speak. Some men just aren't ready, and it takes a major event like a midlife crisis to bring about this realisation. Alas to some it never happens or maybe I shouldn't say "never". Perhaps when we pass on that part is released?

Television was a topic too. Seems I'm the only one who watches it with my daughter on a regular basis. I can see the very good argument for it to be limited and I commend you all for this.

Thanks, Scott, for providing your place/drink and food for this meeting, we just love the atmosphere here.

Next meeting at my place. Tuesday November 29.

HO, guys. Dave.

Dave's Place Nov 29, 2011

The three wise men arrived bearing gifts on what was to be our last meeting this year. Morgan, Roger and Scott came prepared with their 'Secret Santa' gifts, which between all four of us wouldn't be a secret for much longer.

We all sat down at the dining table and talked house maintenance (mainly mowing grass) and rising sea levels (sea levels always the topic being that I'm only one metre above sea level where I live). Morgan explained how the cost of mowers and their maintenance seemed to overshadow the cost of getting someone else to do it. We chatted for a while over cups of tea, Xmas cake, shortbread, crackers, chips and dip, with a backdrop of indecipherable conversation from my next-door neighbours. I had an enlightened moment (without Roger's help) and shut the window facing the noisy neighbours so we could carry on uninterrupted.

Time for check-in so we moved onto the couch and all sat facing the coffee table loaded with lit candles, presents, cups of tea and spirit sticks. Silence ensued as we were at a loss of what to do next … All of a sudden Roger said, "Check-in time!" …

It never ceases to amaze us all of the enlightened intuition that Roger possesses. I mean right at the point when any normal person is faced with complete indecision or doubt they can always rely on Roger to 'come up with the goods'! We laughed and laughed: a good start.

Check-in produced talk about schoolies and their rite of passage. And also holiday plans being that the season is upon us. Also about band promotion and music frequencies, the new level being 432 htz, termed the 'wellbeing' frequency. Talk also about being caught in a job where it's very uncomfortable either to stay or leave: what choice?

Roger discussed a workshop he did on drama and speech (Steiner-based) and we asked him to elaborate after check-in.

He told us how they meditated, picturing first the earth out in space, then imagining the moon circling it, gradually adding all the other planets to create the universe as we know it. He then explained how the teachers talked about a blank canvas and proceeded to paint it with words. Meanings of names by the sounding out of the actual words were discussed; more emphasis was given on the pronunciation though. Very interesting.

Next was present time and each of us eagerly unwrapped our gifts. Morgan was given wine, Scott marbles, Roger a light and I got a teacup. So Morgan can celebrate, Scott may have lost his, but found many more, Roger is the light, and I'll drink to that or anything else as long as its tea!

We also talked about the joys of youth and what it is to be a teenager as opposed to age and the oppression of ill-health.

Time for tea break and we discussed politics; does it really change anything? And the drug problems faced by our citizens in Indonesia with its corruption at the very core of their justice system. The only solution is, if this is a worry, avoid going there.

Many thanks for a relaxed evening, and the realisation that we have over three years of meetings under our collective belts.

Merry Christmas to every one of our men and their families. HO HO HO!

Next meeting at Morgan's on Jan 31, 2012.

2012

Morgan's Place Jan 31, 2012

Present were Morgan, Scott, Roger, Les, Phil, Brendon and I.

Welcome all men to the first of our meetings for 2012.

And a special welcome to our new member Brendon. I would like to thank him on behalf of all of us for his valuable contribution to the night's discussions.

Check-in was a mixture as always.

Everyone is busy yet we have all come from a break known as 'holidays'?

We are all facing decisions—some mild, some extreme. There seems always 'doubt' behind every decision. Does the doubt come from within or is it suggested externally? Can a decision be so consuming that its only judgement is available through the court process? But what if that process is flawed? Can we ever be satisfied?

Moving house has been quoted as one of the most stressful things you can do, yet we all do it sometime or other. It's part of change, which I guess is part of life.

As men we inherit the need to provide, but with that predisposition comes the fear that at some stage we will be unable to. We seek new opportunities and some way of correcting our life balance by pursuit of an income based around what we believe or what we like. To dislike our job or career can be a consuming thought in our minds to the point when it's almost the only thing we think about. Our culture dictates that most of our conscious time is spent in the pursuit of income and there seems no other course of action but to conform.

What consumes us at home? Have we ever considered our conversations with partners, kids, friends, relations and random members of the public? Are they amassed in gossip? Are they really functional? Do they have a point or are they just a banter of entertainment to the listener? What about our internal voice? What is it saying? Is it bickering and complaining all day or is it just enjoying life as it happens?

In all this confusion are we missing the point?

Should our real task be to teach our children? To impart knowledge to the next generation so as to warn them of what's ahead. Or would that be denying them the experience of the world which is forever changing? Are we really responsible for this world together?

Are we not all one?

Meditation: We are so lucky!

Hayley guided us through a meditation and as always did a reading for each of us. We all feel so honoured to receive this.

Toning: Two men were 'toned' and I would like to ask them to write what they felt, if possible. For me it was like another meditation and I enjoy the resonation between our voices. It's also a good breathing exercise and gives us a physical element in our interaction.

Checkout: Checkout was a bit hastened as time was getting late but the Mayan calendar got a mention. So according to them we are all doomed and a few cult gurus around the world would probably agree. Well, we're in it now so we shall see! Mind you, people die every day so for them the world has just ended too.

Next meeting at Roger's Sacred Shed Feb 14, 2012.

HO, guys! Dave.

Roger's place Feb 14, 2012

Five men present to experience the night and Roger positioned us around the remains of a tree stump ringing the fire.

I unfortunately was late and only caught the end of the last man's check-in before giving my own. My arrival disrupted everyone but Roger settled us with a brief meditation. May I say that this was memorable for me as this is my first meeting as a free man.

The discussion was mixed and varied as always. This being Valentine's Day it was interesting to hear each man's dedication to the implications that this involves.

Banana trees became a fruitful subject and this eventually evolved into a group working bee to be held first at Scott's and then each man's place in sequence.

The next meeting will be at my place on March 6.

I deeply apologise for not taking notes and not being totally present in mind at this meeting. Thus this wrap is very brief.

Thank you, Roger, for a great night.

There have been some queries about when we started this group. It looks like it was around March 2008. Greg started the Men's Group online page on June 6, 2008. My first write-up was on Oct 8, 2008.

HO, Dave.

Dave's Place March 6, 2012

Thank you all the men for coming to my place this night: Les, Roger and Scott. In the midst of all the bad weather and flooding and all the other problems we have you still made it!

Check-in unveiled a mix of diet, hard work, self-esteem, depression, court, power, stirring and an umbrella fetish?

However, a common thread revealed itself. That thread was basically 'mental overload'. It happens when our focus is on the problems we are experiencing. Notice I don't say the 'politically correct' word of challenges! As I believe a challenge is something you take on whereas a problem is something put upon you from outside your control. This overload when it becomes almost our entire focus is quite debilitating. It can almost be termed as 'depression'. The effect is to nullify us to the extent that getting out of bed ready to take on the day isn't going to happen. Moreover, staying in bed hoping the day will pass you by seems the better option. But there are so many cultural and societal conditions that we are obliged to honour that we get up anyway and soldier on.

Most of the time even your closest friend or partner is none the wiser. How can they be? They don't exist in your headspace, only you do. But you will find they are very adept at giving you the advice they think you need, cutting through all the flak which they don't realise is there. Each of us exists in the physical universe as physical beings. But there are approximately seven billion beings each with their own thought patterns. Each of these is really a co-joined universe within the physical universe. I guess that's what quantum science is referring to as 'the multiverse', or if it isn't, then it should also be taken into account.

As mentioned by nearly all the men that night, passion is needed to uplift us. What gets us excited? Can we sustain that excitement?

A point to remember: Physical exertion without finalisation ultimately is unrewarding.

There is another point related to this topic of diet. Is our diet just full of too much carbohydrate? Is that a contributor to the lows we experience? Recently many people are switching to high-protein, low-carb and no fat diets with amazing results. May be worth pursuing!

Checkout resulted in a call to Matt but he did not reply. However, he rang yesterday and all is as good as can be expected. We wish you well, mate.

On a separate note I wish to announce that I'll be missing from meetings for a while, probably a few months or more. I never thought I would ever get to this stage but I feel a certain bridge has been crossed with many more to come ... I would like to catch up occasionally but for the time being I need to re-gather myself, so to speak.

I wish all you guys a fantastic journey and thank you for all your help to me from the bottom of my heart.

This may not be the end for me but just maybe a long pause, I don't know ...

HO, guys! Dave.

SABBATICAL

This is the point when I left the group. I had a few visits in the next three years but I only recorded some of them. As you will see they are just poetry. I had reached a tumultuous period when I had to make life-changing decisions. I was going through a vicious divorce that led to court. I also had severe depression and almost took my own life on several occasions.

Of all the decisions I made at that time leaving the group was one of my worst ones.

Realising my mistake, I resumed regular meetings again from 2016 onwards. And still do to this day.

2014

Roger's Place Feb 24, 2014

A Swedish fire torch was our only light
Clouds above us disbursed by stars bright
Four men who discussed over six years of
thought
Have met once again to listen and talk
One confident, one cruising, one questioning
life
The last needs a change, his spirit needs light
One is leaving, such a loss, but to him a gain
The tyranny of distance was always to blame
The once bright Swedish torch almost
extinguished now
Has released most of its heat, its light and
carbon foul
Laughter has filled the air right near the end
Such mirth, such respect, such is life for these
wise men.

Roger's Place Dec 23, 2014

Four men at night
Watching the light
From earthbound fire to starlight bright
Contemplating the world
The dimension they're in
Why can't it be just devoid of all sin
Reaching the past
Realising the present
The thoughts manifest like a mirage in the
desert
A friendship earned
With mutual trust
A perfect evening to celebrate us
A glance through Roger's shed
It's all very clear
Battery power is all the go here
Now walk to your car
With dew-splashed feet
Let's hope it's not long till next time we meet.

2015

Scott's Place Sept 1, 2015

Hi, guys. Thanks for tonight. Here's the best I could do when I got home.

Men round a fire
Observing the light
Feeling the heat
But not here to fight
Nothing to prove
No monetary gain
Baring souls open
Releasing the pain
How easy it is
With like-minded men
To discuss many topics
That inspire no end
Then feel privileged
To share the lives
Of so much experience
Where wisdom resides.
HO, Dave.

Dave's Place Dec 15, 2015

Hi, guys, for the benefit of Scott who's not on FB. Last meeting this year with my Men's Group.

We started seven years ago doing a course in Men's Work called Common Ground. We have met when possible every fortnight since. This group has witnessed such sadness, such grief. But also such joy, such elation. Each man is so different yet we find things in common. The 'presence' in these men helps shine a light on our existence. Who could ask for a better experience? And isn't that we're here for? 'The Experience'.

Merry Christmas to these men and to all who take the time to reach out to their fellow man or woman. Give them a free space to talk. Let's find some Common Ground. Many thanks and love to my lovely wife Corrina who spent the whole day getting the house ready. Then cooking the food for all of us to enjoy.

HO, Dave.

2016

Roger's Shed Feb 2, 2016

Happy 2016, guys.

Plenty of subjects again tonight. I have a bit more time today so here's a wrap-up of the night.

Noise in ears: Roger talked about noisy ears. Something that's been going on in my head for the last couple of years too. Possibly age related or as Roger said damage from excessive decibels in the past. At times the constant ringing can be quite loud. Still not as bad as my 95-year-old aunty. She was woken up last night by a hissing sound, rather like a bearded dragon ready to fight outside her window. Then after listening more intently she thought it was in her room, after a few more minutes of being really scared she realised it was her own breath.

Money on the internet.

Interesting how Morgan spoke about making money via the net. Something I have just been looking at. The internet is such a huge resource. My nephew works for a company putting a system together for universities to track all their students. Taking three years to get it all up and going. But now most of the hard work is done and many places world-wide are asking to use their system. They don't have a large-capacity computer to play and test their system so they log onto Amazon and use one of theirs. Apparently they have around 500 gig of ram to play with so job's done in half an hour.

How long can you ignore your body?

If the body is truth and you ignore it, what happens? I guess the body dies. It tries to get you back to the truth. Its only communication is through emotions and feelings. So if that's true then the body will get sick until you change what you are doing. I hear it all the time. "I am doing this but I know what I should be really doing." "It's killing me but I have to do it to save everyone else." (I do this too.)

That's fair enough if you haven't experienced that problem before. Life is about experience. But if you have then there is no benefit to your life to repeat this. The only benefit is to see if you can shorten your lifespan somewhat to leave room for someone else to take your place. We aren't that overcrowded here yet so please don't do that.

Men's Group Z's Feb 16, 2016

Something different tonight. We decided to meet at Zarraffas Cafe in Maroochydore.

Present were me, Morgan, Roger and Scott.

Check-in showed we're all willing to try something new in our lives. Scott taking three months off work. Roger taking a week's holiday in the Hinterland. Morgan really starting to move on his new business venture. And me having another holiday.

A lesson learned in discussion is not to expect too much from friends and employers. Certain basic moral standards are not always met from those people who should really have a basic understanding. If you let go of the issue, then it'll have less impact on your personal space.

Remember each person is coming at the situation with a quite different perspective. They are in effect operating in a different dimension. Each person on this planet reacts differently inside their heads to you.

Probably better to look at it as more of a miracle if they ever operate on your wavelength at all.

Next meeting March 1. Morgan's Place.

HO, guys. Dave.

Morgan's Place March 1, 2016

It is great to have Morgan back on the Coast again with this meeting being in his brand-new house. Present were myself, Roger, Scott, Matt and of course Morgan.

It was perhaps a sign of the times that all of us were either unemployed, unable to work, choosing not to work, working on our own terms or a combination of all four. The only problem this creates is your personal world fills up the space left for work/employment. Making it increasingly more difficult as you get older to make the transition back.

It was especially enjoyable to have a meditation and reading done by Hayley again. I thought at one stage that we'd lost Roger. He fell in deeply and for a time I thought he wasn't coming out. As always Hayley was certainly onto our deepest thoughts and provided some clarity for each of us. I must admit that Scott looked about 10 years younger. I checked this observation on the way home with Matt and he agreed. Scott, you've made the right decision, mate. Thank you, Morgan, for such a great evening. We honour you and your new direction in life. HO! Dave.

Roger's Place April 12, 2016 by Morgan

Met tonight round a great fire at Roger's house. Few spots of rain and an inquisitive bat were no match for Roger's fire! Check-in focused around a number of topics, including the joys of semi-retirement, and thoughts about our mortality and past behaviour patterns we can sometimes fall into. Then following check-in, the conversation was wide-ranging for nearly two hours—discussions included the night sky, Steiner, music and psychics. Very enjoyable night. Thanks, Roger, for hosting. Great to sit around a fire and look at the stars! Next meeting in three weeks (April 26th) at Morgan's house. HO, Morgan.

Morgan's Place April 26, 2016

Matt, Scott, me, and of course Morgan were present at Morgan's place tonight. Unfortunately, Roger wasn't with us and he was certainly missed.

Check-in lasted most of the night with Matt and I holding the floor to the late hours. We had so much to talk about that we should've split it between two meetings really. Anyway, we finally let Morgan and Scott have two minutes' worth before Hayley took us into a meditation and reading.

It's interesting seeing the law of attraction at work. In two cases, chaos emanating outward and attracting more of the same. The more people that get involved the worse it gets. Till everyone is in on the attack. And I also noticed that the energy of this could be expelled physically. The term 'run it out' comes to mind. So instead of verbalising the frustration, vigorous exercise could be used. Both expelling pent-up energy. Food for thought.

All men have now settled into their new regimes. Either working or non-working, but then that depends on the meaning of work. We are probably always working on something. But this time it's to our own agendas.

Thank you, Morgan and Hayley for looking after us again. HO.

Dave's Place April 17, 2016

Thank you to all you guys for making the trek down south. Lacking a central point, I decided to put a fire on the TV via YouTube. The Fire by the Creek scene seemed best. Everything seemed right for a while until the wood burned down, then it magically replaced itself.

Check-in lasted quite a while mainly because Roger had to catch up with his recent experience with the Love Nest.

Morgan talked about his latest venture which is finally ready to bear fruit. I am still onto share trading which is keeping our heads above water. But it's a bit weird making money by not producing anything, so to speak. The night's talk centred around sex. Or more appropriately, 'making love'. So often not talked about. And also which YouTube screensaver to display on the TV. So good to catch up, guys. Sorry that the flu postponed it for a week.

HO, Dave.

Men's Group April 30, 2016 Dave's Place Eighth Anniversary

Present: Dave, Roger, Morgan, Scott and Matt. At this meeting Roger alerted us to the fact that we are now eight years old on June 3, 2016. Yes, first meeting at Cody's place all those years ago.

The Common Ground introduction night was March 4, 2008. All credit due to Morgan, Scott and Roger. Without these three main players this group would've fallen by the wayside. I have been absent for about one year, perhaps two. I will have to check the dates. But all credit to our three amigos without which we wouldn't exist. Also I would like to credit our men's wives who have helped us along the way. In particular Scott's wife Liz who we have done a course with and Morgan's wife Hayley who helps us with our spirit guides.

Interestingly enough my first channelling session with Hayley was August 12, 2009. Let's look back to that first time we got together: I have a suitcase with most of the info about my experiences during Common Ground luckily so I had a dig. Our Common Ground group:

Stephen, Roger, Cody, Matt, Hein, Morgan, Scott, Greg, David and Colin.

Common Ground Agreements: Confidentiality, Respect, Trust, Honouring, Responsibility, Listening, No Interrupting, Punctuality, Acceptance, All Feelings Okay, Integrity and Honesty, No Substances, Commitment, Sense of Fun.

Our first page of interaction was journey to manhood. What are your defining moments as a man? What did your father teach you? What did your mother teach you? Who are your role models and mentors? What is your greatest achievement? What is your greatest fear? Who is the wisest person you know and why? Where do you belong?

Back to the meeting: As we all find ourselves with more free time we decided to start earlier at 4 p.m. Morgan filled us in on his Amazon job which is just starting to kick off. He has left no stone unturned and I believe he will be quite successful. Scott looks like having more time off after his long service leave. Roger is still working the days that suit him and using free time to explore other avenues to expand his awareness. Matt is thinking about returning to plumbing but not in a full-time capacity. I'm still dabbling in the stock market which seems to be coming up trumps so far. I mentioned that it's time to put a book together about our group.

Secret Men's Business will hopefully be finished this year. The first line will be 'I looked outside to find the blame. I looked inside and found my name.' It's just such a relaxed atmosphere when we get together. Like a band of brothers this ritual is just second nature. It's the second-longest relationship I've experienced. May we have a very happy future together.

HO, guys.

Matt's Place June 14, 2016

Present were Matt, Morgan, Scott and Dave. Roger had the flu.

Matt put on a super feast: roast lamb and vegetables. Much appreciated by all of us.

Check-in:

We started at 4 p.m. which is such an ideal time for everyone, I hope we can keep this. Morgan's business sales are just kicking off and I'm glad we can have a discussion about this each meeting. The stock market is still in its topped-out phase so I don't have anything to report. Matt's about to have a go at plumbing again and it looks like he's scored a good client. Scott is still off work and making himself a priority which will put him on the path to recovery.

Discussion was varied: We talked about 'cancer clusters' and how in the future there will be some 'tell-tale' pointing to why they happen. As yet they are mostly a mystery.

This was the week of the Orlando Mass Shooting in the USA: 50 killed, 53 wounded. We discussed the American gun laws which inevitably led to the upcoming election. Can a gun-loving state really hand in its weapons? Is any up-and-coming candidate willing to put their presidency on the line by saying they are anti-gun? We think not!

Talk moved onto unions and their power over us. Tales of wharfies rorting the system during the Second World War, etc. And drawing a not-so-long bow to the present day when shoplifting, however minor, can be justified somewhat. Is that because we always think it's us against them? The corporations who can afford it versus us who have no say in high-end matters?

Next we conversed on the ultimate shopping mall, whereby your wife goes shopping and leaves you in the 'entertainment area' watching footy, having a beer served by a topless waitress. Coming to a plaza near you, very soon, I hope!

All in all, a great night, thank you to HG for the great hospitality.

See you all at Scott's on Tuesday June 28, 2016. HO. Dave.

Scott's Place June 28, 2016

Present were all five men.

Looks like the competition for the best dinner is hotting up as Scott had a beautiful stew prepared for us. He also fired up the inside fire as the outside temperature was around 10 degrees.

Check-in saw concerns about money again. It seems like the money is there but the access path is a bit tedious. I think patience and paperwork is the key. Depression rears its ugly head again too. I guess it is always lurking, trying to give us its experience. Taking us from the present situation to bad events that really don't exist.

Scott is attending life art classes and I'm sure

he'll be able to persuade some girls along to the next meeting. I'll be boning up on my sketching skills till then.

The financial world around us is reeling from BREXIT. It's an opportunity for some people and a tragedy for others. I like the market turmoil as it's an opportunity to make money. The UK has lost its financial rating and also its prime minister.

We have an election this weekend and the nation seems pretty divided. It's interesting to see the division even amongst ourselves. Having not voted for a major party since 2007 I am always looking for someone to cause some action. I predict a Labor win with shared power to the independents. Morgan has the opposite view and one of us will be $10 richer come the next meeting.

Speaking of which, it'll be at Roger's place on July 13. He will have a three-course meal prepared for us with the first being 'pheasant under glass'. Whilst eating we'll have a parade of naked girlies we can ogle at before the next course!

Should be a fantastic evening.

HO HO HO.

Roger's Sunset July 13, 2016

All present.

We all met at Roger's around 4.30 p.m. Earlier starts still working for us all. Was great to see his beautiful property in daylight for once. And also to admire all his solar panels which occupy the majority of his roof space.

Roger suggested we witness the sunset down the road but first he had to light the fire. Opening the valve on a nearby gas bottle he lit the protruding pipe and a roaring flame gushed out. Picking up the bottle he aimed it at the fire which immediately sprang to life. At first I was unsure what he was doing but after witnessing the obvious benefits of this method I asked if he'd do it again on video. That's now on Facebook for all our friends to comment on.

Anyway the sunset-viewing paddock was five minutes by car so Morgan offered. Five people in the Prius meant it was now lowered sufficiently enough to get admiring glances from any nearby bogans. It scraped its way out of the driveway and back again. Morgan didn't need his exhaust system anyway; battery power from now on.

At the sunset viewing Roger proceeded to

enlighten each one of us as being as beautiful as the vision splendid on the horizon. And with each passing moment it became more intense. Such a depth of reds, pinks and yellows with dark clouds around the perimeter with Mt Cooroy as its matter.

Check-in had a common theme of siblings problems. Mainly their perceived body image. It's hard to portray our knowledge to an individual who perceives they know more than we do. Especially when they believe it was different in our day. Then we have to balance our advice so it doesn't look like, "Do as I say, not as I do" ... Drugs are always an issue too. There are so many types out there now and I guess more readily available than in the past.

But I'm not really the right person to comment as I don't drink and have only had a puff of a standard cigarette only once in my life. So my experience in this subject is very limited.

We also discussed the future of the 'workplace' and how the travel time to each job now can entail half the working day. With traffic so congested there must be an easier solution to travel chaos.

The election has finally been resolved. What looked like a hung parliament has now resolved in a clear Liberal win of 76 seats. So I had to pay Morgan $10 and eat a slice of humble pie.

Speaking of which, Roger presented us with a lovely Kitchari protein stew. That coupled with the roaring fire made for a wonderful evening.

I honour him for all his effort this night, thanks, mate, HO.

Dave's Place August 8, 2016

We had another early evening get-together, this time at 4.30 p.m.

Roger had to quit work early and Morgan drove everyone down (except Matt) so thanks for that effort. The rest of us are exercising safe work practices. Basically avoiding normal work altogether. All men present.

After a cuppa I drove all the guys down to Golden Beach to take in the view before dinner. Unfortunately, the weather wasn't ideal. The wind was rather strong and cold so after 30 minutes we pulled the pin.

Back home we had time before dinner for two check-ins; Matt and I fronted up.

Dinner was a stir-fry that Corrina had planned for us with coconut rice that went down rather well.

After dinner, back to the lounge room and I put the fire on via YouTube. We finished our check-ins and after some discussion decided to give Scott a toning. Matt wanted one also so we obliged. I must admit both toning welled up some emotion for me. I hope that these toning's have done their job. Please feel free to tell us.

Discussions as always were varied.

Donald Trump seems to be a topic every meeting lately. And worldwide he certainly has interested many media outlets. Probably won't do his business model any harm. As for the wider community, only time will tell.

Dreams were another topic. It's interesting how each man has such a different experience on this level. Probably attuned to the fact that we all exist in different dimensions.

Good to see Morgan is on the money with Amazon. He's really kicking goals. Roger is enjoying the interaction at work and has spotted a Tesla which is on his shopping list. Matt is off to Perth soon with another holiday in October. Scott had hardly any reaction to his last treatment which is a sign that he's getting better, I'm sure. And me? Well, same old thing, playing the share market. Weekly income is increasing though, so happy about that.

Tomorrow is Census night, so don't forget!

HO, guys. Next Meeting: Monday August 22, at Scott's Place.

Scott's Teepee Sept 15, 2016

Different meeting this time. We started at 10 a.m. at Scott's place.

Matt and I were met at the door by Morgan and Roger then led down the secret bush track to Scott's giant teepee. Fantastic setting surrounded by bush so very secluded and quiet.

Scott had a table set up for refreshments and food and we initially sat around the fire pit on various sized log slices.

Morgan had just been to Tonga and swam with the whales, one of which almost took him out. Matt had just returned from New Zealand, just clinching a real estate deal. Scott is about to head off to India. Roger is off to Melbourne and I'm not going anywhere after the stock market collapse. However, I had a good experience earlier this year so I've had my turn.

After a while we decided to enter the sacred teepee. Bit warm in there as the sun's heat came straight through the fabric. But the open flap made a difference by allowing air through via convection.

Each man seems to be experiencing things outside their comfort zone. Change is happening to all of us at different speeds and it will be very interesting to see where we all end up by Christmas which is drawing nearer.

Unfortunately, I had to rush off and take Matt with me so the meeting only lasted 2.5 hours.

HO, guys.

Roger decided to do his own write-up.

Here is my write-up, post Matt and Dave leaving the meeting early. Well you didn't leave early, we just stayed back late.

Dave was on a tight schedule and was pushing Matt to hurry up as it was cutting things a bit fine to get to his next appointment. Dave walked ahead to give the hint to Matt that it's time to go and after some final communications Matt shot off up the track in pursuit. After that I went and had a piss in the bush.

Scott, Morgan and I proceeded to get a cuppa ready to sit around the outdoor fire pit to review matters of importance. I grabbed a big handful of snacks, I never did perfect the art of Breatharianism. What seemed like a long passing of time while munching, talking and pouring drinks, Matt comes running down the track and out of breath to pick up his sunnies that he remembered were left behind on the banquet table; I thought Dave will be fuming having extra delays!! That made me laugh, sometimes I have a bit of a chortle at other people's expense and misadventures. Although, Dave may have been very centred and equanimeous of mind while he awaited for the return of his forgetful fellow traveller. Knowing only too well of the story of the farmer and his son:

A farmer and his son had a beloved stallion who helped the family earn a living. One day, the horse ran away and their neighbours exclaimed, "Your horse ran away, what terrible luck!" The farmer replied, "Maybe so, maybe not. We'll see."

A few days later, the horse returned home, leading a few wild mares back to the farm as well. The neighbours shouted out, "Your horse has returned, and brought several horses home with him. What great luck!" The farmer replied, "Maybe so, maybe not. We'll see."

Later that week, the farmer's son was trying to break one of the mares and she threw him to the ground, breaking his leg. The villagers cried, "Your son broke his leg, what terrible luck!" The farmer replied, "Maybe so, maybe not. We'll see."

A few weeks later, soldiers from the national army marched through town, recruiting all the able-bodied boys for the army. They did not take the farmer's son, still recovering from his injury. Friends shouted, "Your boy is spared, what tremendous luck!" To which the farmer replied, "Maybe so, maybe not. We'll see."

The moral of this story, is, of course, that no event, in and of itself, can truly be judged as good or bad, lucky or unlucky, fortunate or unfortunate, but that only time will tell the whole story. Additionally, no one really lives long enough to find out the 'whole story', so it could be considered a great waste of time to judge minor inconveniences as misfortunes or to invest tons of energy into things that look outstanding on the surface, but may not pay off in the end.

The wiser thing, then, is to live life in moderation, keeping as even a temperament as possible, taking all things in stride, whether they originally appear to be 'good' or 'bad'. Life is much more comfortable and comforting if we merely accept what we're given and make the best of our life circumstances. Rather than always having to pass judgement on things and declare them as good or bad, it would be better to just sit back and say, "It will be interesting to see what happens."

Finally, after some further communications with the remaining group, Matt bolts up the track again to reunite with the awaiting Pajero.

Settling in around the fire pit on the log seats we could get back to matters of importance: just as the 400-ton whale's tail's left fluke was about to crush Morgan to the bottom of the ocean there was a sudden eerie hush that came over the remaining group! Slow, deliberate steps could be heard deep in the bush undergrowth just as the sky was growing darker and threatening with rain approaching. The steps came closer, then only to stop; something was there, well camouflaged: a sniper with a rifle? Hearts beating in chests we sat in silence, frozen in fear!! Further steps and crushing of the undergrowth, hard to determine the exact direction: what emerged down beyond Scott's vehicle was a huge four-ton Varanus priscus, thought to be an extinct monitor lizard with a massive tail similar to a whale, with the two flukes connecting in a V-like appearance, able to crush its prey. I thought of Morgan's close encounter with the whale and that we could have that happen here on land. Scott reassured us that she was friendly and not to worry; at that moment it casually moved on down towards the lower swamp lagoon area.

Morgan took a sip of his cuppa and said HO; Scott in between snacks talked about his upcoming family holiday in India: amazing!

That reminded me of a story of an Indian Boy Named Saroo Brierley.

Saroo was born in India. One night, when he was five, he went with his older brother to scrounge for food at a railway station. He fell asleep in a train carriage which carried him away while he slept, across the country, to the huge city of Calcutta. Saroo found himself alone, with nothing but what he was wearing. He lived off the streets before being taken in by institutions. He was then adopted by an Australian couple, and brought to their home in Hobart. Nothing at all was known of his birth family. As an adult, Saroo began the near-impossible task of using his childhood memories, and Google Earth, to locate his lost family in India.

The film based on Saroo's story, *Lion*, will be released in Australia later in 2016. I don't think I could watch the movie but the story interview with Richard Fidler I felt was heart-moving as would be his book *A Long Way Home*.

I was about to tell Morgan and Scott what happened when Saroo got back to India as an adult, and then it started to rain so we packed up the table and filled the car with all the cushions, etc. out of the teepee. I finished the story and we signed off and headed up to the house to depart ways. In jest, HO, Roger.

P.S. Thanks, Scott and Kaitlin, for a unique venue. Thanks, Morgan, for suggesting the morning time slot; a novel first for the group.

Impromptu Meeting
Tuesday Oct 4, 2016

This was the meeting we had when 50% of us weren't going to have one. As I'm writing this it's best explained from my angle.

Corrina and I had just finished lunch on Hastings St. Noosa. It was about 1.45 p.m. and I had briefly spoken on the phone to my mate Max in Victoria saying I'll get back to him after lunch. Corrina and I have been struggling lately with the hard facts of life, being we had cash going out and none coming in. So after being on a stringent diet of doing nothing for two weeks I allowed us to have one day out.

We were on the Spyder which I had just spent three days figuring out where to fit rear indicators as the hard pannier bags from the US I ordered two months ago when I wasn't cash-strapped had arrived two months early. The Yanks don't have rear indicators because they use flashers in the tail lights. Our laws do not allow for red indicators so I had to retro fit some. Anyway, good excuse to go for a ride!

So we finished lunch and walked back to the Spyder and I asked Corrina if she'd like a coffee before we moved on. With that the phone rang at 2.00 p.m. "We're here," said Scott. "Where is here?" I answered. "At your place for the meeting …"

Instant panic followed and my mind went into overdrive trying to figure out how the meeting arranged for 2 p.m. on Thursday suddenly jumped two days forward. What followed was approximately 60 minutes of phone conversations between Scott, Matt and myself. The upshot being, as Scott and Roger said, "We should've arranged this through Morgan."

Apparently Matt and I were on the same page. Scott and Roger were on another. Confused by the fact we used emails and texts which didn't meet certain criteria.

Anyway, as luck would have it we all met at the Coffee Club Cotton Tree around 3.30 p.m.

First up, Scott is looking good. He'd just had a massage and informed us it hit the spot (must get her contact details). He also said his lead levels were way down so his treatment is working. His holiday in NZ sounded great and although quite cold I envied him being amongst all those hot springs.

Speaking of looking good Roger had a great holiday down south and I believe this is just the start of his travels. Overseas for you next time, mate.

Matt is about to go on 'The Horny Goat Tour 2016' so is resting up, gaining all his strength.

Me, I'm throwing everything at Amazon with my book. Having freebies and adverts going on Kindle as well as Facebook. Thirty free books went out in the last day so I hope that reviews will follow soon after. Also I am back into the stock market, buying at a good price and waiting for the swing back; so far so good. As I'm writing this I have received an email from Kindle saying they have paid money into my account. As all the books have been free I can't see that I am due anything. Weird … but they say it'll be in on Oct 5 so I'll wait and see.

We discussed many things as usual. But of mention is the housing market which most people have done pretty well out of. How long will it last?

I did flag that I'm going to present a marketing campaign to one of the local bookshops. Offering a free Spyder ride with every book sold. Still looking at public liability issues and council objections with that one. Mind you, the lads seemed enthusiastic.

As for my indicators … the rear tyre wiped one out coming home as I didn't allow enough room for when the shock absorber bottoms out. Bummer!

Anyway, onward and upward, men.

And as Roger has just said, "Success is not final, failure is not fatal. It is the courage to continue that counts."

HO, Dave.

I propose next meeting at my place Tuesday October 18, 2016. Please let's get this one right or else we'll have to ring Morgan to take over.

Roger's Place Nov 3, 2016

Well, after six weeks away Morgan is back and will be busy organising us for the next couple of meetings before we all call it quits for yet another year.

His business is still powering ahead which I find quite inspirational. He mentioned that all is well now he's back home and that's because he had a good house sitter. A good house sitter is as mandatory as planning your actual trip, especially if there are pets involved. To arrive back finding your house clean and tidy and your pets in good condition really caps off your experience abroad.

Speaking of abroad, Scott will be off again this month to India. Like Morgan he'll be six weeks away including Xmas in a foreign land. Should be amazing.

Roger remarked how he had a symbiotic pain after witnessing his brother's problems after heart surgery. I have experienced this also and it's very real. He's almost doing full-time work now which must be a shock to his system.

Speaking of which, I, 'Dave the unemployable', have got to the sticky end of my savings and applied for 'Job Start' with Centrelink. I dragged my reluctant (not really, but that's what it felt like) wife along to register also. So stay tuned to see if it's possible.

Speaking of wives, which we inevitably do, I wonder at what point they actually become aware of the mindset they're in and how it affects us? How are we ever expected to read the mind of the unreadable? Or gauge the silence as something we have done wrong. Or, is it all just a play with control? Some things I guess I'll never understand.

As Scott said, the event is just the way things happened. The interpretation of that event attached to emotion means the truth just went down the toilet ... well, words to that effect.

I'll leave with Roger's quote on money.

Money can't buy

Wisdom

Appetite

Joy

Friends

Peace

Health

Beauty

Loyalty

But it can buy an 15K beautiful robot doll that has half those attributes ... and more thrown in ... (he didn't say that last bit).

Thanks for the great night, Roger, and the exploding pressure can. Good effects!

HO till next time at Morgan's ... two weeks.

Morgan's Place Nov 15, 2016

All present.

This is the second last meeting of the year. Scott will be off overseas to India soon so will miss out on the next one.

Trump entered into discussion as he is still a major worldwide topic. Most, if not all, media outlets around the world including America got the presidency wrong. How can this be possible? Doesn't the media represent the people? Or do they just represent themselves? Are the media as influential as they think they are? Trump won not by just a small percentage, more like a full-blown landslide. Is he the beginning of world change? Is there a shift to the so-called 'right'? It's certainly happening in other countries. Who will be the next government to swing by his way and take control?

The discussion also centred around North Africa. Morgan, Roger and Scott had all been there. Interesting how society is almost totally different to here.

Matt had a great holiday. Lost a tender. Battled the storm (I heard that story yesterday). And copped a sore arse from too much time on a bike seat. Well, that's what he told us anyway.

Roger is still working full-time and by all accounts his taxes will be paying for the rest of us; well done.

Scott is looking good and says he's over the nauseous period of his treatment which is great.

Morgan's heavily into exercise and his business is paying dividends so all is good. I got lucky over the weekend and sold another eBook which believe me is quite a shock!

Everyone copped a good toning tonight and I invite you guys to share your experience on here. I'll collate them and put it all together later.

I had a real head buzz, which is usual for me. There was a full-on shower of consciousness pouring through me and it got caught in some of the crap in my head on the way through. I was getting knocked around quite a bit. I think I finally cleared up at the group hug in the end. It settled my head noise down. My consciousness is quite crowded. And it probably needed more time to clear up. But an enjoyable experience as always.

Thank you, and HO, guys.

Next meeting 6 p.m. Tuesday November 29
at a fish 'n' chip shop, Coolum Central.

Coolum Meeting Nov 28, 2016

Morgan, Roger, Matt and Dave present.
Christmas soon
The year's at an end
Our world is in turmoil
And not on the mend
In biblical proportions
With mozzies, flies and moths
And shaking the foundations
Of the pacific rim troughs
But our earth is not alone
To accept this fate
Trump's voted in to give us a shake
Market forces I'm sure will sort him out
Then we'll all breathe easy
Till the next nut plays out.
So here we are staring at the 17 gate
What is there left to contemplate?
Getting older but wiser is in doubt
"Who the fuck cares?" I hear you all shout
If experience matters
Then we've had our fill
2017 is already in the till

David Zachary Smith

So let's get the cash out
And splurge out on life
Do something wonderful
Don't worry about gossip
Or the daily grind
It's all too involved
And takes too much time
Here's cheers to the future
For our group of men
Let's live Heaven on Earth
And share it again.

2017

Morgan's Place Feb 7, 2017

Great meeting at Morgan's place. Such a relief to walk into a house with air conditioning. And the spread courtesy of Heather was much appreciated by all. This year will probably be the hottest on record and it's certainly taking its toll on all of us. Knocks me flat from lunchtime onwards.

All men present for our second meeting this year. Good to see Scott back looking like he visited the fountain of youth in India. Reporting he's reached a realisation and is fired up to get back into work from next week. Roger looking good as always. Matt's getting into exercise. Morgan had a good health report. And I'm seeking motivation.

Topics including Trump, of course. He's the topic right around the world every day. Can all publicity be good publicity in his case?

Movies had a mention and *Lion* certainly sounds like it creates an emotional reaction. Whereas *La La Land* seems to be a bit off with the fairies.

Scott read part of the *Bhavagad gida* book and the section about 'non-attachment to outcome' struck a chord. Good insight for all of us.

Towards the night's end Morgan's cat talked to us and the dogs joined in to share a biscuit. I took a traveller for the drive home.

Very enjoyable night. Thank you, Morgan.

HO, guys.

Next meet at Matt's Place.

Tuesday February 21. See you there!

Matt's Place Tuesday Feb 21, 2017

(Revised with help from Scott.)
Down on the waterfront
Wind roars
Clouds manifest
Mullets splash
Man with no direction comes free
By practising non-attachment
And releasing thoughts with no substance
Life in transition
Purpose, routine and work
Let no man be untouched.
Dave.

Scott's Place Tuesday March 21, 2017

The big fire night.

Early start at 3 p.m. so we could participate in a 'Burning of the Heap' ceremony by Chief Fire Warden Roger.

(Roger's prose.)

How do we catch the spark? How do we nurse the flame? How do we light the fire?

Observe and experience fire in the world, then awaken to the transformative power of fire in our hearts, in our inner life and becoming.

There is a 'fire of love' which we long to enkindle individually and in community.

Luckily no one caught fire and nothing evil raced or slithered out from the burning mass. So we retreated back to the house to be baptised.

We also had a birthday celebration for Matt who made the big 50 the day before.

Check-in produced what seems to be almost an immutable fact that all of us seem to be under some sort of financial pressure. The cure seems to be buy this book: *The Barefoot Investor.*

I for one had a long list of the usual complaints but they all just drained away under the peaceful surroundings and excellent company.

So it was really a peaceful night. We had a swim, excellent food and rattled on about movies, etc. till 8 p.m.

I felt so relaxed there I could've just lay down to sleep. So I believe I should honour Scott and his family for creating that beautiful environment that we experienced. And Morgan for bringing the birthday cake.

HO till Tuesday April 4 at 7 p.m. My place.

Dave's house April 4, 2017

"I lost my power in this world, because I didn't use it." A great line from Lindsay Buckingham's song 'Go Insane'. Fleetwood Mac.

Power: who has it? Who has control of our lives? Do we have it? If we do, how do we use it?

Each of us has a power or energy story tonight. Whether it be women's energy which feels very draining. Or men's dominant energy that can only be neutralised by attacking back with the same or more force. Unless you have an ace up your sleeve.

If someone exhibits power over you how do you manage that? Do you pander to it, or fire something back?

If you have nothing to lose then let all guns roar away. But if you can't sustain a loss then look for the ace. It'll be there, hidden behind a facade of bullshit. What's the lesson to be learned? I guess be careful of your own power. Try not to harm others but be aware of when they're harming you.

Play the game, look for the ace. If you get a chance leave the game altogether.

Something to ponder.

HO, Dave.

Next meeting, Scott's on April 18.

Matt's Place May 23, 2017

I arrived early to give Matt a rubdown (as always) and to prep him for the evening ahead. As part of the prep session I questioned him about all the topical events such as sport, radical Islam, *Bomba the Jungle Boy*, and made sure he had the latest goss on Trump. We did this in the kitchen which for all intents and purposes was quite normal. Except I had to dodge a peculiar item hanging off the kitchen pulpit that can only be described as a goldfish death bag. Then just as we were nearly at the climax his phone rang and I gathered by the half conversation that the rest of our troop (F) were lost.

I raced outside, releasing my iPhone from its sheath, hitting the iTorch app, thereby releasing the SOS feature which flashed an emergency beacon that the guys would recognise. And so they did. Spotting me from the far corner of the road they quickly advanced to my position. The troop alighted and it was greetings all round.

Moving inside, the troop were first shown the dead fish bag which became the first quiz of the evening. I saw an opportunity to gain more thoughts on this subject so I posted a pic on Facebook entitled WTF.

Each man decided lubrication was in order and with that took position outside, facing the canal. Except for me as I sat side on, thereby missing (unbeknownst to me as no one mentioned it) the nudie prod games that were displayed in the houses opposite. Must've looked like a large screen telly locked on the porn channel. Anyway, I had to be content with the odd mullet splash, not to be confused with any bogan memories.

Talk ensued as always, only being interrupted by the odd choccy or almond mix biscuit blocking the throats of its assigned cannibal. Caravans and travelling got a fair bit of air time which for most retirees is the holy grail of pensionerism. That's as long as free camping sites are liberally spread around the country. That'll all change when the government finds a way of taxing them.

It's interesting to hear about women's conversations, as in they rely on gossip, rumour and innuendo. Whereas us blokes it's all about fine art, poetry and golf! Why is that? And why are we subject to micro-managing misandrists? Who really cares? I think we need to discuss the real problems! Famine pestilence death. The end of the world is nigh. Seems everyone is hurting at this time.

Financial pressure, back problems (which is also a financial condition which manifests as support) are very prominent in our discussions tonight. Almost every man had a tale of woe about that subject. But we're not alone, even the stock market is having a hernia. The old adage 'Sell in May and go away': I wish I had heard and heeded that last month.

Flies are in full force around the coast. Everywhere I go people are complaining about them, hence Matt's kitchen mobile which is meant to ward off the bastards.

We are collectively being flogged with depression or anxiety and without a defined cure. And because of the perceived pressure we can snap. Often at the people closest to us.

Roger enlightened us with a song to cheer our hearts and pep us for the next day. That was a welcome break. I wonder if we could share a song each, one that really touches our soul. I know I have a couple.

But right at the meeting's end Scott had an answer. PNG. Present 'N' Grateful. If we can hold our minds clear enough then the moment bears no harm. Who would've thought the answer could be so simple …? Like me.

Many thanks for Master Matt for providing the place, food and refreshments. Just remind me of the view next time, okay?

So PNG, men.

HO till Scott's place, June 6.

PS. I'm not gay! Toodles, Dave.

Scott's Place June 6, 2017

Our weather system has finally turned. Cold air but beautiful, clear days, such a contrast to that bloody hot summer. But riding with the cold air is a sickness, manifesting as bronchitis, flu and other chest infections. Unfortunately, enough to hospitalise some.

Preceding our meeting Scott had been emailing us all week about his work situation. Basically he's being bullied by a boss on a power trip. How do you handle these bastards? It's possible to just tell them to fuck off, but you can only risk that on a fellow grunt. But what if they're a few rungs higher on the ladder, how do you handle that?

There was also an element of anticipation amongst us. A vicious rumour had been spread about the possibility of Scott doing the first check-in. Scott always checks in last. But I do recall years ago when he didn't. I think his contribution at that time was one word: "Pass". Upon hearing this Roger was so amazed that he threatened us all with the song 'Black Betty' if Scott actually went through with this threat.

Whatever happens this promises to be an extraordinary evening.

We eased into the night with some light banter. World economics was touched on. Trump has made even more gaffes and that's hitting our economy hard. The Australian share market is tanking badly. Amazon is coming and local listed retailers are being severely dumped. For example, Myer was as high as 1.25 in April but now it's 86c. Worse still it listed in 2009 for $4.10. And I bought some! WTF?

After a time, a hush settled over the room.

We waited with bated breath.

Would Scott go first?

He reached for the stick.

Coughed then hesitated.

And he breathed his first word!

Roger immediately sprang to life and sang 'Black Betty'. A rendition to rival Ram Jam's best unplugged version. I was undecided whether to video Roger or administer him a sedative. But just as fast as he exploded into verse he stopped, allowing Scott to continue.

After hearing Scott's story, we continued the discussion about workplace bullies. One particular item involved their cars. Brake fluid, gravel and potatoes down exhaust pipes. Prawn and squid juice injected into seats. And various pungent liquids poured into the phlegm vents. All good stuff!

Morgan the entrepreneur looks like he's out of the woods and Matt is looking at a Jim's franchise. That's the asbestos, not the Jihad one. Morgan was talking about the franchise fees when all of a sudden a mouse trap went off. Is that a sign?

Roger is into yoga. Quoting prices: $17 or $20 for 1.5 hrs. Good stuff, especially for backs as this seems to be the catalyst for other problems.

Roger mentioned that Scott going first felt wrong. I agree. Like seeing the end of the movie at the start.

Back to normal at my place. Tuesday June 20. Don't forget Morgan's 'calm app'.

HO HO, Dave.

Dave's Place June 20, 2017

Dinner ended up being the main event. Corrina made a lasagne al forno the day before after scurrying around everywhere for the ingredients. Then it was time to cook. At 5.30 she asked when the guys are coming. I said

5.30. A quick check of the meal which had been in the oven for 45 minutes revealed it was still cold in the middle.

Panic time!

Turn up the oven and hope the guys are late. And they were except for Matt. And he didn't mind. During the meal sun spots/ skin cancers were discussed. Dry ice is the usual cure. Black salve was talked about. We have a pot in the fridge which has yet to be used.

Morgan brought along his brand-new bar coolers that will be hitting the retail stores soon. He's also got projects with other retailers on the go.

After dinner we really only had time for a check-in. Then tea break and a checkout.

Our TV backdrop was a beach scene that repeated every five minutes. I for one thought it was too bright. I reckon the fire was better. Would like your thoughts.

We all seem to have a struggle with work-related issues. Which is interesting as approximately a year ago most of us weren't working, if I remember correctly.

Roger is a part-time worker. Scott is still working part-time. Matt is looking for part-time work. Morgan's part-time workers have to lift their game. And my part-time work is causing high anxiety.

Roger is right into Enneagrams and I guess at one stage we should test ourselves. Scott is giving his kids the chance to express themselves through art. Matt had a reading which has reinforced what he already knew.

I've finished my book and the guys suggested professional editing. Morgan is looking forward to an overseas holiday ASAP.

Libido was briefly mentioned but there wasn't enough time to raise the issue any further.

PNG, guys. Dave.

Morgan's Place July 4, 2017

The start of the new financial year and also Tom Cruise's birthday, but he didn't get a mention.

I rolled up to Morgan's and the door was open. Inside light conversation centred around investing in the stock market. Morgan's going to invest some super money on Aussie stocks and Roger is looking at the next big thing being Tesla. We made tea and started tucking into Heather's cake, then Scott arrived.

Morgan started us off with a meditation via his Calm app. It led us through breathing and body presence.

Next, check-in.

Roger has been quite unsettled. His gut advising him it's time to buy Tesla shares. Interesting how he has been annoyed constantly about this. Is this intuition kicking in, or anxiety masquerading its own focal point? I hope it's the former.

Morgan has really done his research with Amazon and has produced an income stream with all the bases covered. Manifesting the dream.

Scott feeling better at work with the pressure from the hierarchy backed off.

And me. I'm feeling out of sorts. My book is mostly done and proofs are ordered. I'm considering professional editing but I'd like to recoup the expense. That means having a book that people want to buy. Self-doubt rears its head again.

We briefly discussed humanity's future. How long will we last? What will replace us? Had we already created our replacement? Is there a new consciousness out there, silicone based, using the Internet as its brain?

As always time will tell. HO, guys.

Next meeting at Roger's on Tuesday July 18.

Roger's Place July 18, 2017

Sub Title Matt's Soapbox

I picked Matt up from way down south and headed north in anticipation of another good old yack around one of Roger's fires. Upon arrival Roger's neighbour seemed to have the same idea with the flames illuminating half his trees. Roger must've felt the competition from next door as his fire was unusually large. I reckon four trees were sacrificed, enough for a week's worth of camp-oven dinners.

Roger led us through a guided meditation through visualisation first up. Then it was check-in time … for Matt with very brief interspersals from the rest of us till we just all gave in. Whether we held the stick or not it made no difference. Matt recently returned from Singapore and had plenty of tales to tell. And every time someone else checked in it reminded him of something else to say. So after his five check-ins it was all over. So briefly, Morgan told us he was busy, I talked about my upcoming book, Roger is watching his Tesla shares and Scott was remembering the good old days at Woodstock.

After check-in we discussed how human it is to compare yourself to others. Especially in monetary terms. Yet the comparison is a mental lie as each person literally cannot tread the same path. Your life is owned, operating from the particular dimension your mind operates in. Do you really want to live someone's else's life anyway?

Truth reared its head and has been discussed at length in other meetings. Can we really own the truth? Can you tell someone the truth, wife included here, without being torn apart for doing so? Is the truth really just unacceptable? If so, then how long do we continue dancing around it? Even at funerals the truth seems whitewashed somewhat. A complete bastard to many can be a real saint to the few. All about perspective, I guess.

A.I, as in Artificial Intelligence, was conversed at length. Does it have the capacity to take over all our jobs? The manual ones are a given, but what about those that need creative thought? Take that a step further and will the AIs end up with their own consciousness? Where does that leave us? It's going to be a very interesting future!

We also had a collective conscious thought about the meetings with a real fire. It just seems so natural. Outside in the elements seems to be so much more relaxing, so neutralising. Pity we can't have one at every meeting.

Next meeting at Matt's place, Tuesday August 1, 7 p.m. Burn some furniture, Matt!

HO, guys. Dave.

Matt's Place August 1, 2017

Travelling along the main road to Matt's place, I followed a Toyota Prius. I didn't click it was Morgan's with the rest of the gang inside. That was until within 200 metres of Matt's house and the Prius stopped in the middle of a T-intersection. Aha, I thought, that's Morgan. Anyway, I turned left and Morgan went straight ahead. No problem as Morgan will take the next left and he'll be there. But not so, as I then saw him go straight ahead just as I pulled up at the driveway. I guessed he was doing the tourist drive, showing the lads all the top spots and attractions. A few minutes later, having exhausted all the local landmarks, he arrived.

Matt greeted us in the usual way. That is, not recognising any of us and questioning what day it was. Having leapt that hurdle we alighted and went inside to cups of chai tea all round. Scott peered out the glass door towards the lake and stated there was a fire outside. "No bloody way," I said, unless it was a fake one. But no, I was wrong. Matt, the selfish bastard, had fired up an iron pig, force fed by lethal carcinogenic timber from Scott's hazardous waste leftovers. Leaving me, the holder of the next meeting, having to better that somewhat; shit!

Before check-in we discussed the group's roots. How we got involved. Were we the first Common Ground in QLD? That conversation then moved onto various men's courses we had done, including sweat shop and nudie ones. Morgan mentioned about a NSW event whereby three people topped themselves afterwards. Which begs the question, how are they addressing this now with all our extra nanny state laws?

The check-in stick almost worked, with only

mild interjection as compared to last week. I talked about my book cover photo shoot and how my life has completely changed since we started Common Ground. Matt is heavily into exercise and also helping Scott with his new house. And interestingly had a great response to his van advertisement via Gumtree. Roger stated that Matt reminds him of his girlfriend; I'll leave that there. And had a penetrating interaction with an Aboriginal elder lady from Arnhem Land. He experienced a fall at work which luckily didn't cause an injury.

Morgan is forever busy with his online work and weekend footy. He stated how this affects his relationship in the negative. I have experienced this as well. It takes some adjustment when you're always around your wife. It's hard to get 'clean air', so to speak, when you want it. Always a bloody compromise.

Scott just shook off the current flu/bacteria virus attacking the coast and did so in only two days! He had a remedial foot massage by the same Aboriginal woman as Roger, said it was very beneficial. He also took the interaction one step further and had a painting party which many people dropped into. His mission, paint the Messiah!

All this time Matt's mate Brian (giraffe statue) sat silently watching us. I thought he was a bit close to the fire but he didn't flinch. After more gasbagging and various innuendos we took off inside for another cuppa. I told the guys to read my book as there will be a series of questions to be answered at the next meeting. Get any answers wrong and you won't be allowed to check-in. Scott, as you didn't get a copy your turn will be the meeting afterwards.

I hear Scott's new house is nearly finished. Looks like it's going to be some sort of international brothel. Big money spinner. Good luck. How much, by the way, just in case someone is enquiring?

Next meeting, Dave's Place, Tuesday August 15. HO HO.

Dave's Place August 22, 2017

Special preparations tonight as I prepare for the Secret Men's Business exam. The guys have been busily studying my book, *Secret Men's Business,* for a month now and I expect they are brimming with newfound ideas and hallucinations.

With all the questions and answers formulated it's now up to the guys to fight it out to determine the winner. The winner will go on record as the highest graduate from the SMB university. Leaving here with the knowledge that of all the people who know more than most others, he'll be one of them. Brings a tear to my eye just writing that. The losers (everyone else) will go on with their prosperous lives, seemingly unaware of what they never had before they lost it.

Corrina has baked a special cake loaded with calories to keep the blokes awake while I interrogate—no, sorry, assist—them with the test. Washed down with copious cups of tea, I believe that this combination will do the trick.

I've set up the exam (lounge) room with the TV tuned onto a YouTube rainforest scene. Hopefully it'll reduce the stress of the evening.

The guys arrived and Roger turned up with one of the proof copies. Could he be the one who takes the prize? Unfortunately, Scott couldn't make it but he found a way to participate. So after some brief banter, food and drink we adjourned to the lounge room. I had a USB hooked into the telly loaded with 10 questions and a view of the prize for first place, a large set of jugs. Each man was then given paper and a pen to write their answers.

So then heads down and it was on. NAPLAN test for kids had nothing on this examination. I had set aside one hour for the test which surprisingly only took five minutes, such was the dedication of these participants.

Morgan finished first, way ahead of the crowd, absolutely gleaming with confidence. Roger was visibly under pressure and Matt was stressed to the max, the reason being we were soon to find out. So, after five minutes it was 'pens down' and I swapped everyone's pages around to minimise cheating. With the answers now on the big screen it was a fairly simple task for each man to mark the papers.

Answers were quite varied which loosely translates that most were wrong. With 13 points on offer the guys were fighting it out head to head. Roger scored 2.5. And Morgan was way ahead on 3. Scott scored 3 as well which was the reason Matt was so stressed. He had been channelling Scott for the test and was having trouble deciphering his answers. Thus Matt, who forgot to do his own test, came last with 0.

So now came the sudden-death playoff. Morgan and Scott were locked at 3 points each; who would win the jugs? Grabbing the book, I quickly searched for a question that a three- to five-year-old could answer easily. Asking "What is the character Scott's actual name?", Morgan fired the answer right away. So with a grand total of 4 points Morgan won the jugs.

Check-in. Roger is being very careful in his relationship with other workmates. Paying attention to how he is perceived. Matt is clearing junk from his factory, physically and metaphysically. Morgan is really busy with his business which requires a ton of research. And me, well, it's more of the usual.

We didn't actually check out but had a lengthy discussion about ashrams in India.

Next meeting at Scott's, September 5.

HO HO. Davo.

That's all the meetings up to the publishing of this book.

EPILOGUE

OKAY! I hope by now you have a much better understanding of a Private Men's Group. The interaction is such a great benefit that I encourage you to start your own.

Not the standard barbie involving a piss-up, but a real down-to-earth, honest talk about yourself. Listen to your fellow man. Allow him the space to really open up. This then gives you breathing room to do the same. At this stage of your life you'll really benefit, believe me.

Life is too bloody short!

ABOUT THE AUTHOR

David Zachary Smith has authored seven books so far with two more currently under way.

Basking on Insanity Beach, his first book, is about suburban domestic violence.

The Secret Book of Life is about what you basically need to live.

The Secret Book of Nothing is about that.

The Secret Book of Life's Choices is simple explanations for your decisions.

SCI explores the depth of consciousness. A rare insight into the basic thread of life.

I Am You follows a tormented life through a web of intrigue that comes to an unbelievable conclusion.

Thank you for reading **Secret Men's Business**.

DZS can be contacted through his website: davidzacharysmith.com

Made in the
USA
Columbia, SC